T0195930

Eternal COMPANIONS **L**OF**VE**

FRANK SCOTT AND NISA MONTIE

BALBOA.PRESS
A DIVISION OF HAY HOUSE

Balboa Press books may be ordered through booksellers or by contacting:

Balboa Press
A Division of Hay House
1663 Liberty Drive
Bloomington, IN 47403
www.balboapress.com
1 (877) 407-4847

Because of the dynamic nature of the Internet, any web addresses or links contained in this book may have changed since publication and may no longer be valid. The views expressed in this work are solely those of the author and do not necessarily reflect the views of the publisher, and the publisher hereby disclaims any responsibility for them.

The author of this book does not dispense medical advice or prescribe the use of any technique as a form of treatment for physical, emotional, or medical problems without the advice of a physician, either directly or indirectly. The intent of the author is only to offer information of a general nature to help you in your quest for emotional and spiritual well-being. In the event you use any of the information in this book for yourself, which is your constitutional right, the author and the publisher assume no responsibility for your actions.

Any people depicted in stock imagery provided by Getty Images are models, and such images are being used for illustrative purposes only. Certain stock imagery © Getty Images.

Print information available on the last page.

ISBN: 978-1-9822-4131-5 (sc)
ISBN: 978-1-9822-4133-9 (hc)
ISBN: 978-1-9822-4132-2 (e)

Library of Congress Control Number: 2020900571

Balboa Press rev. date: 01/21/2020

Contents

Preface

Love

When the Love comes down
From on High,
Take it—receive
The Essence
Like a delicate Rose
Heart—blossoming
To bring Love's fruition.

The fruits of God's Blessings
Are Myriad:
Loving relationships
Continuing throughout eternity,
The breezes of heart-opening
Compassion blowing across

Centuries, eons of cooperation
Until each, precious Living Being
Stands up
Within him or her Self
To acknowledge the fact that
All is God;
All comes from God;
All returns to God
In an infinite, unbroken Wave
Of Love
Turning every heart
Into the brightest lamp,
The most Radiant Star
Of His Grace and Mercy.

There is nothing else but God—
Above, below,
Left, and to the right,
Within and without,
For we are nothing
Without God's Godliness.

His Goodness within
Shines forever
As a beacon on every shore—
Listen, listen
To the inner melody
Of our Creator's Whispering Song—
Allowing each of us to arise,
Sing from the Heart,
His praise
Forever and ever—

There is One God only
Whose secret, nameless Name
Encompasses all names and forms,
Transforming
Each Soul-possessing,
Spirit Being
Of Light

Into His most humble servant
—the lowest of the low
Lifted to the very highest
Station.

The Glory of God
Always.

"Turn the light on, so I can see!" calls out a young man as he enters the living room.

"It doesn't matter to me," his elderly mother, sitting with his father, tells him. "I can still _feel_ the warmth of the sun, coming in through the window, although I can't see well." Her son remarks,

"Light or no light, I still can't find my way."

His father, says gently,

"If it doesn't matter to you, one way or the other,

you must be of those that follow others. Why not let your Soul's Knowingness lead? Then your world will be bright and full of colors. You'll meet lots of people from different places, talk, and learn so many things."

Oh, reader—*How is your world*?

Revelation

Looking into the mirror
Another Self gazes back—
Cleaner, sweeter, purer.
Behind that Self, another peeks,
Emerges and another...
Allowing God's Sight
To See It-Self.

This Self is all we need:
Without time,
Wholly present,
Illumining Oneness,
Releasing
The little, baby self
From crawling around its own axis.

Please, God, Reveal a drop
Of the crystal Joy of Thy Love
Within us
As you whisper softly,

"I Love you"
To each
Of our Selves.

Belief and unbelief address a fundamental level

of the existential experience in a world like ours,

expressed throughout a linear and non-linear aspect of time.

Linearly, throughout every day and circumstance when we are face-to-face with others, our present rolls into our past, frame-by-frame, leaving the memories cherished as the evidence of our interactions, the value of our relationships.

Non-linearly, when we are alone, we continue to experience, within our mind-world constructs, as we connect and communicate our thoughts and feelings with all life.

Our joy and satisfaction, or discontent and gloom, our faith in others and in our-Selves and our Creator—or lack of it—all spread through the level of the Spirit. These ideas surface and flow outwardly, fifth-dimensionally, seeding the engine that manifests, from a non-linear state into a linear flow, transforming into a future that rolls by, becoming the past—as part-and-parcel of a Whole within.

Belief defines and sets one's degree of confidence and acceptance that evolves, over time, as one's Faith in something, be this a certainty in our egoic-self or our True Self, believing in a Creator or no Creator. This creed or these ideas grow like seeds, as each of us continually adds to them, so that they grow into a future bringing its observable results to all who experience them.

The questions emerge: *What determines* the existence of mind-worlds within a larger Mind-World? How do our lives reflect the resultant dreams—or nightmares—within the larger collective of the Dream-World interacting within itself in a state of *Oneness of*

Being and Manifestation? If one were to choose among the countless mind-world constructs of all entities, would one choose those filled with positive and constructive ideations, or those lacking such virtues?

Ultimately, all traveling entities believe in something or somethings, even when it gets down to a singular point of reference—Believing or having confidence in one's self. Even at this level of Self-trust and Self-acceptance, this single idea feeds one's existence, at the most basic level of life and intelligence, allowing each of us to see how important and crucial this information is. This belief or idea transforms itself into the continuing flow, enabling humanity and, indeed, a civilization, to rise as a Whole.

By examining how dependable, honorable, accountable, and constant we are—representing the assurance and certainty we experience in relation to our Higher Selves, the Reflectors of the All-Knowing One—we can determine how continuous will be our advancement and that of our civilization.

When the latter belief in the Godliness within is lacking—when we are disconnected from our Soul-based point of view through incorrect thoughts, feelings, and actions resulting from the evils of corruption, exploitation, debasement, degeneracy, manipulation or perversion—then our spiritual evolution, as individuals, and as a society, is stymied.

We, as a political corpus, are responsible for the downfall of our civilization, as our species has failed in its moral and ethical duties by not living and advancing our shared future in accordance with the Divine Plan of God for His creatures.

In situations *where the belief in something good* vanishes from the heart of the traveler, that entity is assured of his or her downfall. The same societal downfall takes place as the number of such disbelieving entities grows. The effects upon society bring disruption to its continuing means of advancement, taking away the assurance of peace and tranquility for all. In a process similar to when illness strikes a healthy bodily system, an unbelief in the effects of goodness results in the decomposition of what were prevalent qualities within individuals and society as a whole: orderliness, functionality, and clarity of thoughts and actions that appease the heart and organize the mind.

Unbelief is masked under a set of falsehoods, a state of heart encircled by agnosticism or atheism, dissent and distrust, and an incredulity towards there being a Purpose for the individual or for us all.

Our potential-in-transit, a vastness embodied as an expression of a Oneness of Being, at the Heart of our humanity, becomes incarcerated within shaky mind-world constructs, ineffective and unconvincing in the Light of a Truth whose warmth even the least aware should perceive.

How do we feed the growing needs of our hearts as we grow older? The answer is to use our ability to bring in greater aspects of the Whole that surrounds and embraces us non-linearly, beyond the domains of our minds.

The thought-forms that feed our growing mind-world constructs require a constant flow of new information to fasten securely the new mental structures brought in by the flow of the experiences we have. There is no stopping for as long as we live and are a part of a world of time. The existential experience goes on and on, disregarding physical death, for it is only a door to another world of time.

When the heart is open, there is so much more to living. When the heart is kept pure, the mystical experiences come and reveal the richness behind and beyond a world of time's physical details within the domain of the mind. Live, then, as a complete entity without the egoic self's material and mental burdens saddling your heart. Allow the flow of Soul-revelation to take you to a glorious encounter with your True Self—and the Beloved of all the worlds of God.

Realize the importance of your beliefs as part of your system of Life and Intelligence, that when integrated with other systems of Life and Intelligence, contain a greater portion of God's

Blessings. These Blessings seed, here on Earth, a Kingdom both everlasting and beautiful, the like of which no Earthling has yet experienced.

We are living the _Greatest Lie_, and most don't even know it. We are existing within lives without the Creator, Whose existence we deny, and Whose Will and Pleasure we ignore, and act against. Denial and resistance, arrogance and the mismanagement of our passions, have manifested from our hearts and minds, turning a potentially beautiful opportunity to live on an Earthly Paradise into many wasted lives existing upon a planet whose inhabitants are dying unnatural deaths.

Wake up, then, and smell the roses hidden—but growing—in the garden of your Heart!

Without the Love of God

The Longing

Deep within the recesses of the heart
Is the longing for God.
Nothing else will satisfy.
The Soul, like a child, searches
Everywhere
For the Unknowable One
Until He, She, the Divine
Parent, whispers,
"Come. I am here, within,
Always here—Patient
For your return."

Suddenly the Heart is uplifted,
"I'm not alone!" The Heart says.
So the journey ends
Where it began....
In the Heart's Knowingness.

Be thankful to the Longing
Leading us back to Our-Selves.
Hop on the ship of Intrepidity,
Sail by the wind of Primal Cause,
And the Destination
Is easily reached.

Then let the tides of Forever
Gently land the Soul's vessel
On the shores of the True Self,
In the Land of Revealing,
Where the Chosen Ones gather—

Faces up-turned to bathe
In the Sun's rays
Of ebullient Truth
And all-embracing Love.

What's the true Source of Love?

Is love that which is derived from our physical passions? When we say,

"Let's make love," what do we mean? Can we actually claim to bring love into existence? Does love exist between our extremities? Are we confusing that which is sustained by our sexual energy with Divine Love?

Can we tell the difference between the Love of God as Source, and our hormonally-generated feelings of sexual attraction, infusing a euphoric moment?

It is the Love that is eternally Present that gives us true nourishment—allowing for eternal companionships filled with the Joy and Gladness of Spirit, two Light Beings adorned with an ever-present bond that defies our minds and our understanding of Earth-bound relationships. This Love has only one Source—our Creator.

Are we not its recipients?

The Fountain

Wealth and poverty
Mean nothing when
The Treasurer's at hand.
Loss of life
Cannot be counted
When the Life-giver
Births Souls

From the distant
Land, filling
With Joy each Chalice
Of each Being
Manifested—Beyond
The infinite leaves
In the ancient Forest
Rise the drops of water
From the limitless
Fountain
No one has ever
Counted.

How We Grow

If God were to reach
Inside your Heart,
What would He find?
The Rose of Love
He planted, with soft

Petals to caress?
Or would He prick His
Finger
On a bramble's thorny nest?

They say there's a road
Less-traveled
Where only the wise
May go.
But often it's the foolish
Who find—and stumble
Down His path—
Hearts lit by the stones'
Rosy glow.

It takes less time
Than a moment
For God to plant

His Wish—
That each of His treasured

Creatures
May follow the way
He's lit.

There is no doubt,
'Nor was there ever,
Of the Path
To not depart:

Plant Divinity
As an oak,
In the acorn,
Of the Heart.

Are the world's inhabitants feeling the Love of God, or its absence? In order for the Love of God to come into one's heart, justice must reign in one's life. Righteousness, honesty, fair dealing, open-mindedness, and a lack of prejudice need to be present in the individual's heart.

The relationship between the male and the female of the species, from time immemorial, has never seen the light of justice, fairness, and truthfulness. It is time to look at this relationship, and discuss its ramifications, for it has afflicted, and continues to afflict, almost all the women on the planet.

Onwards

Our winged Soul's journey continues
Past the last breath
Of mortal frame,
Free, spiriting
Towards the Unknowable.

Ha! We laugh,
"So everything was just
An illusion."
The Garden here is beautiful—
Light,

8

Bird songs, plants singing,
A cheery squirrel
Passing me a nut
To put in my pocket.

In God's timing
<u>Love</u>
Makes beauty grow.

Release

Beyond the first rainbow of Life
Is the second, colored arc of dreams,
And beyond that,
The third Vision of Possibilities,
Until the colors merge like waves
In an ocean of Beauty
That cannot be imagined—

Except by the Creator;

Or by Joseph, when he first
Slipped into the coat,
Bright with rainbows,
Woven together
With God's Love.

What are we
But dots of Light,
Stars caught
Within spinning galaxies,
Until the Infinite One
Releases
And drops us,
Still spinning,
Onto the Plane of Oneness?

What is it with our addiction to, and obsession with,

our sexuality, and what it represents, that it justifies

everything we do? Men have compartmentalized this aspect of their existential experience, and have never looked at it. Sexuality gets used merely because it is there! We don't think about its purpose beyond the pleasure derived from it.

The result of ignoring its true purpose and proper use is agonizingly painful to describe, as written from a beginning that has no beginning. The women, representing over half of the population on Earth, have been, painfully and without a choice, subjected to the abuse and violence resulting from this warped expression of _love_. Women have taken this load, a saddle that keeps them, for the most part, incarcerated as genetic machines that dish out copies of ourselves, time-and-again. Men, especially, disregard the discomfort and the birthing pain, the relationship itself, all in the name of business as usual. Without concern or thought about the much larger content, the purpose and significance, within the Simulator and Trainer, of our eternal companionships, entities known as *human* lose the value and direction of, and for, our Light-Beingness—beyond this short-lived, mortal experience.

The imbalance and unjust treatment of over half of the population has continued for millennia, so that today we experience a social order completely dislodged and disconnected from its Higher Purpose. Our vain attempts at having long-lasting and meaningful relationships are but unattainable dreams, erroneous facsimiles of what our eternal companionships could be like—were it not for the culture and understanding rooted in unfairness and abuse.

It Takes No Time

Beyond the last line of Light
On the horizon
Is a whisper
Of the Unknowable One.

Fall back into the Self,
The pool without ripples.
Look everywhere
In the Sun-infused
Space,
Until everything dissolves
Into nothing.

"Here I am, my Lord,"
You say to your-Self,
Standing, now,
Under the spreading Tree
On the wide-open
Plain of eternity.

It is, of course, Spring—
Birds flying nearby,
Butterflies floating,
And the air with a hint
Of something indefinable,
Delicious.

The Center Where All Things Are Born

A whirlpool circling
Into a point
Opens up onto the Plain
Of Oneness.
How many lives have gone by
Before we realize
We've been here before—
On a planet
We're destroying.
And yet—it's simple

To change the view point:
God is One, Lord
Over everything.
Why not ask within for Direction,
Swirl past destiny
To cling to His Mercy and Grace?

The point of no-return
Is also the way back.

When the Love of God is absent, meaningful objectives appear without consequence, and meaningless aims are full of import and worth. The traveler's aimless search to those that Know is but a stage, one of many, as the Loved One lies still hidden.

A Gift of Sight

The silent
Big Bang within
Reveals the universe
Contained inside
A point
Leading to the Soul's
Secret tunnel.

When the gray, gauze curtain
Is drawn back
A lovely Garden appears
At the far corner of our bedroom,
To the right of the window
Where the green, quilted Chair sits,
Holding my folded clothes.

These two worlds are One:
The one we see, touch,
Made of mortal dreams;

And the One, God's Dream for us,
All Light and Beauty,
The Garden—
Sprung from our Hearts.

The world we each experience and live in, the universe within, as we observe it and understand it, as we each experience it as a separate, fractional and temporal, existential experience in a world of time, differs from others' worlds, as an expression of what lies deep within each of our hearts.

These omni-dimensional and multi-directional expressions of worlds-within-worlds, representing myriad desires, entropic in their nature, each come to an end, as we awaken elsewhere, time-and-again. Such is the Simulator and Trainer, allowing for endless expressions of egoic-selves, travelers

17

incarcerated by their own vain imaginings and ignorant of what should be: a world of Eternal Beauty, continuous Joy and Happiness, allowing us a completely new way of perceiving, understanding, and experiencing Life.

Unlike the myriad expressions of worlds of time within the Simulator and Trainer, worlds of desire and ignorance that cannot be integrated to become the One Experience we are all having, at once and always, the *Eternal Realm offers just that, an integration of systems of Life and Intelligence, coupled to the One Love that Reveals to all beings the Blessings and Gifts of the Spirit*.

It is the Love of God residing in each heart that is the One element transforming our heap of dust into Paradise. Our separate existences are superposed upon by the Beauty and Joy flowing *outwardly from within*, coalescing all these disparate and separate existences within worlds of time, dissolving all of our impressions and misconceptions, chimeras and deceptions, false semblances and appearances of lasting relationships, into the *Eternal Companions of Love* that were always meant to be.

This transformative process infused with the Creator's Power is found within the Word of God as delivered and dispensed by His Latest Manifestation—bringing about the Return and Resurrection spoken of since ancient times. This process repeats itself, time-and-again, throughout the Simulator and Trainer, whenever our separate and disparate, fractional and temporal, existential experiences have expressed mind-worlds that run counter to His Will and Desire, antithetical to Unity, creating the present risk of self-destruction for our species.

There is no time to be lost in Returning to the way it should be—in becoming the Reflection of His Will and Pleasure, rather than the will and pleasure of His creatures. The Resurrection that speaks of our reconnection and quickening, the _turning-on_ of the Heart and Soul-based state of awareness, is a necessity for our clear functioning, our ability to reflect and express the perfections found within our Selves. Through this Oneness of Being, we experience the transforming power to express and Manifest this Oneness. We thereby participate in integrating all of our worlds into One Universe—as an Eternal, ever-advancing Civilization built upon eternal companions of the Love of God.

A Hurting Heart

To come across so many travelers whose hearts have been hurt, and whose healing needs are so obvious, leaves those that know of the Divine alternative with the memories and faces of the many incarcerated Souls now living paralyzed lives, with dreams that have been turned into nightmares.

In the midst of each of these tragedies, we discover the absence of belief in anything that is good, and therefore in the Source of all Good—God.

Ironically, each such traveling entity ends up blaming God for having allowed the action or the actions that others perpetrated on them, when the true culprit resides within the creature's disobedience to the Rules of the game of life, and the pervading ignorance and prejudice, the injustice, that keeps the Love of God from reaching each entity's heart.

Once the disbelief in God has taken hold of the heart, the way of a quick recovery is shut.

Lord, give me Your Eyes, give me Your Ears, give me Your Voice, give me Your Hands, give me Your Feet, give me Your Mind and Heart, so that I can see with Your Eyes, hear with Your Ears, speak with Your Voice, touch with Your Hands, and walk in Your Ways, filled with beautiful thoughts and feelings, while eternally living in Your Love.

Within Each Blessed Being

The Sun's effulgence
Shines on all—

The blades of grass
Poking their pointed heads
Up from the soil,
The curving oak branches
Stretching their massive arms
Across the blue-sky air,
Even the flit-fluttering
Monarch butterflies
Roaming from bud
To flower.

Just so, the blessings of God
Rain down upon every soul—
Deserving and undeserving—
Showing that in God's Day
All are One.

Lifting our hearts
Like sunflowers leaning
Towards the August rays
Of the afternoon sun,

Warm and comforting,
We can release
All worries and doubts,
For God's Intention
Is that each one of us
Be brought closer and closer
To His Divine Embrace.

Soon, there is nothing
But that Love,
Infusing every second
With infinite, indefinable
Grace.
Glory to God in the Highest,
As Peace
Rises from each hallowed heart.

The One

Poverty and wealth
Are relative—relating
To distance or nearness
To God.
I am poor when my heart
Sails far
From the Eternal One.
I contain the Infinite
Treasure when I clasp
Close to me
That Oneness
With All.

The illusion of separation comes
From feeling with-out
God with-in the Self.
The Self's Image and Beauty

Of the All-Powerful One
Is never separate—
Only ignored.

Let's welcome
The Radiant Self
Within, the Heart's
Hidden Treasure unfolding in
The richness
Of the Voice within,
The Blessings of Spring rain
Beating open the petals
Of flowering Souls
Who listen
Intently,

"I made you rich In My Love.
Do not squander it for gold.
I made you wealthy
In My wisdom.
Do not discard it

For worldly honors.
I made you immortal.
Choose not to forget
Thy Treasured Self
By wallowing in the dust
Of temporal desires.

I made you full of wonder
Like a newborn child.
Live eternally in gratitude
For our Oneness."

Forgiveness

On the long road
To the Highest,
Many stop-overs occur:
Resting by the Well
To quench one's thirst
With the Divine draft
Of Love and Wisdom;

Pausing by the Gate
That opens onto the fields
Of Wildflowers—each a Soul
Saved by the Grace
Of His Majesty;
Breathing in
The Immortal Fragrance
Of Illumination
While ascending the steps
To the Palace
Of Living Understanding.

Yet when the final Door
To the Unknowable Essence
Is cracked open—letting
In the thinnest sliver
Of golden Light—
We collapse
Into the dust,
For only the Grace
Of God's Ever-forgiving

Glance
Can lift our hearts,
And raise our eyes,
To the All-Mighty One's
All-encompassing
Smile of welcome.

Oneness

Without God
We are nothing—
Dust in the wind,
A ray of sunlight
When a cloud-burst comes,
A raindrop
Sinking into the wet earth.
How long have we forgotten
The Source
Of our existence?
Painted horses rising and falling

On a carousel, we long
For release from our
upright, wooden poles,
Our encircled lives
Re-happening
Through centuries
Until we dissolve,
Fall back,
Into the pond of Light,
Embraced by the Mystery....
In the dissolution
Is the re-appearance
Of our-Selves.
From nothingness, then—
Everything.
The Soul's Wonder
Laughs at illusion,
Living
The soft brilliance
Of immortality
Simply bestowed

Upon us
Like the Sun-Light
On impossibly-transparent
Mountain waters.

The entire Simulator and Trainer is either an Ocean of individuals consciously aware of the Beauty of the Kingdom, or just conscious of their surroundings, be these near, or far away. They all reflect their unique knowingness and understanding through actions upon a world that physically incarcerates the Soul in a theater-like stage, moments and aspects of their existential experiences shared in a physical plane, within the myriad conditions that represent neighborhoods, families, work places, geography, languages, rituals, and traditions.

It helps us to see the Simulator as an immense

ocean holding all players everywhere, and always, each immersed in a differing place and depth of understanding within a world of time. As each traveler transits from one to the next state of Being, he or she ages and moves on to another plane of existence, carrying a Oneness of Being and a degree of Manifestation. Each increasingly reflects the higher qualities and spiritual abilities, or their absence, the higher or lower understanding reflecting one's relative nearness to the Beloved of all the worlds, and expressed as one's vision of— and effect upon—mortal realms.

Some of these travelers live and experience this world, but reside Elsewhere—fully identified with the Soul and expressing the True Self. Others totally live for their desires derived from a limited world of time.

Those that are advancing in nearness to the Beloved are hardly understood as they speak the melodies of another Realm. Their hearts are rhythmic pulses of this Love that they embrace and welcome. They see this relative world from a different point of view, and they act upon it in totally different ways. The vicissitudes of life do not damage their hearts, for they are Blessed by the nearness of Reunion. They are filled with hope and life, as they serve their kind.

Within

Why not let go the past's illusion?
Let it run downstream, washing away
The mud of useless regrets
For misguided choices.

All streams are useful, beautiful even,
Veins of water
Feeding the ocean's
One Heart.

This morning the rain
Descends with purifying power,
Soaking every leaf,
Puddling the grass.
The lizards are invisible
In their arks of twigs.

It's a perfect time to relax
Into the high drips, low whooshes,
The rush-from-the-sky sounds
Like His Voice, weaving, spiraling
Into a single Point
Of Light.
Suddenly—
All the clouds scatter.

Throughout all our mortal lives, we wake up and dream again.

Thousands of times, perhaps more. All of these dimensional realities are superposed into one reality—the one I share now. I don't know how long it will last, or when I will see a certain person (or other forms of life) again. If it is meant to be, that entity will be in my dream of life, again and again. Lives come and go. "Here" means anywhere, at any time. The past may repeat itself, or it may have a different ending with a new purpose never before experienced. This new _present_ exists where the former dream, in a different time track, used to play its scenes.

During a life time, we may change tracks of time, and dreams, more than once as we "awake" and "die" spiritually, our Soul-based viewpoints changing dimensions (or stations) in an imperceptible, timeless manner. Each time our lives re-start in a new dream taking us elsewhere, or not. In the end, taken together, all of these experiences speak to us, giving meaning and fulfillment to each and every traveler in worlds of time.

The significance of returning to the True Self, and being resurrected of the Spirit, comes to mind when it needs to, as each of us pries open and breaks a veil keeping us conscripted in our understanding. Thus, the new dream within a Dream becomes a part of a library, the scroll of one's existence, while walking the path laid within a world of time, and again, in some other world that looks like this one, except for minor changes that only those versed in mystic knowledge discover just in time, not a minute too soon, or too late.

Thus, O brothers and sisters, we ask that the *Light of God* illumine our way, keeping us in the straight path, of pure and tranquil heart and clear mind. We ask the Creator of all these worlds to bless us as seekers of the Truth, staying the course that brings certainty when it is needed most, guiding us past our egoically-created nightmares, the loops repeating within worlds of time, so that we may live God's Dream for us—filled with virtues and overflowing with Joy.

Pray to Remember and Return to your True, Immortal Self—superposed upon your temporal life—and not to be lost in the myriad twists and turns of the labyrinth of existence that incarcerates the unwary traveler.

Beyond the Shores of Time

Before the people lost their way,
They understood
How to live:
See each living thing
As part of your own body.
Let the grasses in the meadows
Be your hair.
Let the rivers be your veins,
The fish your blood cells.
Let the air be the breaths
You share,
An extension of your-Self,
Like the limbs reaching out
From the trunk
Of an ancient Tree.

*

Let thy- Self be planted
In the soil of Remembrance,
In the void
Of Great Mystery's
Endless Will.
Let the infinity of Light
Flowing from the stars
Be thy Heart's Radiance
Whereby you touch
Everyone, everything,
With grace.

*

Let gratefulness
Ride thy galloping Spirit's
Knowingness,
Expanding time, smoothing
The sandy shores of Self,
Until you glide
Within the curling, cresting
Wave of God's Dream
Onto the Shore of Perfections.

Without the Love of God, the Heart is always exposed to the vagaries and deviations from the Truth arising from one's egoic-self. We cling to our vain imaginings, and follow all our desires, and not once do we raise our eyes to thank the Lord of all the worlds for continuing to give us the time to discover His guiding hand in the midst of so much error.

The Heart is the precious seat of your Soul; do not sully and defile its sanctity. Let God's Image, the Source of all good, rest in its midst.

Let the Love of God infuse your life with all goodness, helping to reveal the significance of one's Self in the midst of one's family and community, and further, value and enjoy the all-embracing envelope of a world family immersed in the same Ocean of

God's Love, free from all the encumbrances that keep the heart empty and without life—a blinding condition blurring all existence.

Listening

Across the ocean,
Beyond the sky,
Within the heart,
Lies the Infinite Mystery.
Call to the One
Oneness Who Lives
Beyond time,
As the baby bird
Peeps for its mother.
You _will_ be answered,
Easily, softly,
The way butterflies move
On the breezes in spring.

As each earmarked experience comes down the stream within our tracks of time, so do the resources and alterations required to succeed. We can recognize these opportunities as necessary for our spiritual growth, despite their apparent incongruity and incompatibility with our relative existence and our limited understanding and material or mental aims. These experiences need to be completed, for they bring about the required transformation, furthering our understanding of our True Purpose.

Herein lies our greatest challenge: to resolve the seeming conflict between our personal desires and the Will of God—by surrendering to His pre-ordained and pre-recorded Path for our sojourns in a world of time.

Since all good comes from God, this divine Path

allows each of us to Remember and Return to each one's Immortal Self—fully guided by the Soul-based state of awareness—and leaving the Simulator and Trainer altogether following one's awakening.

Rise and Let Go

Gaze at a rainbow
And you will observe
How the colors effervesce
Into white
Light.
Just so our Selves
Merge in the Unity
Of God's Grace—
A Oneness
Of Purpose and Intent.

How long has it been
Since we remembered
That we light up
The same sky
From the same Soul's
Sunlight
And moon-beams?
There is no separation,
One entity to another.
Our hearts are one
In the point and line
Of eternity.

Find within
That Land
Where the Ocean of everyone
Meets the shoreline of Self,
Gently surrendering to the Divine

Like a wave rising,
Descending, water particles
Sinking invisibly
Into the sand.

The whole universe is there to teach us to love one another, and learn about the wisdom that brings balance and harmony to us all.

Love is about balance and harmony, about sharing, giving, and receiving. Love is about feelings of joy and belonginess, about being here, connecting, and caring. Love is life, and life gives us back Love.

Inner Conversation

At the top-most point of the mountain,
Where the air is clear,
The Soul's Understanding

45

Of the Great Mystery
Flows down like rain
From pregnant clouds
To the valleys:

"Behold. I have brought to you
A verdant Earth upon which
Bright Beings live.
Why have you disregarded
My injunctions
For peace and harmony?
Why have you rained down
Destruction, disease, and
Iniquity?
Is this how you answer
My All-powerful Love?"

Rising from the depths
Of the heedless people
Comes a silence—
They neither hear,

Nor listen.

So the Creator
Turns His Face
Away from His creatures—
Briefly.
The world hurtles itself
Into the abyss
Of unknowingness.
A few creatures cry-out,
"Save us, dear Lord."

In His Mercy, again,
He extends a hand
Of Grace.
"My beloved creatures.
Though you have abandoned
Me, I will not abandon
You.
Though you whisper
The faintest cry for help,

My Grace roars out
Like a lion.
For I am the Unknowable
Essence, the depth of
Whose Grace and Mercy
No one may know.
May you, My creatures,
Be of the thankful,
Always,
And forever."

The Language of the Heart

Ideas govern who we are and who we think we are. They bring concepts into play in everything we do. Ideas are born from our minds. Influential, fourth-dimensionally, in the world we live in, and conditioned by our genes, the environment, and our experiences, our mental programs can bring the whole into view in good ways, or bring inaccurate, partial representations of reality with negative consequences.

Feelings tell us how we are responding to Life. The Heart governs the fifth-dimensional state of

Life and Intelligence, the Spirits in the universe. These forces bring into view everything everywhere: attraction and repulsion, growth and instinctive intelligence, the rational faculty, and the Spirit of Faith—all exist within the spiritual heart—the seat of the Soul.

The mind does not work alone. It depends on our sense-perceptions to bring inwardly everything that exists outside. When we pay attention to something, anything, we are importing that information to within our-selves. Thus, we deal with two of the four worlds, or domains, the worlds of the senses and of the mind, that we need to import our information of a Whole that represents everything that forms the actuality all around us—the way things are.

The other two worlds, mostly absent from people's conscious awareness, are not available through the senses or reached by the mind. The third world is that of the Spirits of the universe, or forces, as imperceptible fields of activities, representing and acting as the pre-cursor engine that manifests, and expresses. It appears as intuition, accessible through the heart—a realm of feelings. A domain that is non-linear, without past, present, or future, as well as holding bi-directional, carrier waves connecting the higher and lower realms, the world of the Spirit allows our Soul-based state of awareness to move freely anywhere in time and space.

A more accurate language needs to exist for us to understand properly the world of the Spirits of Life and Intelligence. This language would bring into the linear world of material constructs an understanding of the realm operating through non-linear time—a mystical world dressed in symbolism.

The fourth world is the domain of the Soul. The Heart is the seat of our Soul-based state of pure awareness. The Soul contains the engraved image at the root of who we are, through which the Creator reveals His Beauty—the Face of the Creator, and the Divine Plan for each of the creatures, or entities to see It and reflect.

Here, too, our language needs to include words expressive of this broader point of view. This language best describes our Source as that which knows a beginning in our Selves, but does not know an end, in the Creator. This Soul-based condition is mostly aptly delineated as an eternal flow of revealed, existential experiences that unfold who we are.

We need to start here, in the Realm of the Soul, and begin to point to the definitions that best describe all of us, always, and no matter where we may find our True Selves to be at any given moment in a world of time.

Thus, we are entities, as Beings of Light—subjects of illumination or enlightenment. We are also Soul-possessing—that which allows us to see and hear creation with the Eyes and Ears of our Creator. We are Spirits of Life and Intelligence—that is, endowed with those imperceptible fields of activity that give rise to the powers of attraction and repulsion, growth, instinct, rationality, and Faith. *Here, Faith represents a sense of belongingness and relationship to everything, slowly growing as a state of Knowingness and Lovingness that fills one's heart.*

We are also seekers of the only Truth—that the Creator's Will and Pleasure is carried out on whomever He Wills. We are potentials in transit and transcendence—ever-changing and trans-dimensional. And, above all, we are eternal companions and members of an ever-advancing civilization that knows no boundaries; we are meant to exist in a oneness of place, mind, heart, and Soul.

When the Heart is closed and inaccessible, we are disconnected from two sources of information: our Soul-based state of pure awareness, and the Spirits of Life and Intelligence of the universe we are visiting.

Thus, the vast set of information and resources we require does not reach us, affecting the carrying out of our purpose, and our comprehension of the significance of this fractional and temporal, existential experience. Therefore, we fail to grow in understanding and Love, delaying and prolonging our journeys of exploration and discovery, and jeopardizing, as well, our stays on a planet of time.

Without a Heart connected to the Spirit, we miss feeling the immensity of a fifth-dimensional state, and unifying and translating into words and ideas the beautiful ornamentation existing in Realms otherwise beyond our reach. Instead, we experience a life that is incomplete at best, marred with discrepancy, imbalance, impermanence, and disharmony.

These higher dimensional domains exist; however, we can't access them without attuned hearts. Without being connected to the Spirit of Life and the Soul-based point of view, the Heart, the seat of the Soul, cannot allow us to enter the tenth-dimensional Realm with its marvelous revelations in store for each one of us! We are thereby prevented from experiencing the good and the perfections of the immortal realms in the here-and-now.

Thus, we live experiences that come and go, fraught with the fleeting happiness that fails to uplift our Spirits, or touch the Soul, that doesn't reach far enough within, leaving us feeling empty, in search of something we can't describe or have. What's more important, we can't conceive of, or experience, the goodness, wonder, and beauty of True Creativity upon the shores of consciousness.

Each and every Soul-based virtue may birth myriad creative and useful thoughts. These concepts translate the Heavenly Beauty into actions, supported by Divine Wisdom reflecting a transformative process that securely bonds the hearts of all into a Oneness of Manifestation assisted by One, harmonious Mind.

Released from the Womb

New birth requires emptying,
A letting go to Source.
We are nothing but dust
Until the Great One
Animates us with the Fragrance
And Beauty of Divine Love.
The Unknowable Essence
Is a contradiction:
We know of that Oneness

Within our own hearts.
Let the Love
Stream forth—untamed—
To every cell of the body,
Every member
Of creation,
In sparkling, joyous
Waves.

Ya Baha'ul 'abha
May the Glory of God
Be with thee.

How to Find Love

Within the innermost Heart
Of the Universe
Lies the point of No Return:
No return to worlds of time
Where nothing lasts;
No return to the suffering

Based on false and useless
Desires; no return
To separation from
The Beloved One.
Yes to union
With the Unknowable
Essence—Life of the Spirit
Bubbling up from the clear spring
Of the Soul!
Yes to innumerable realms
Of Grace, the bestowal
Of the Lord's righteous plains,
The lands of plenteous
Virtues and total surrender
To His Will.
Yes to God's way;
Yes to Immortal Love,
Eternal Wisdom,
And the Embrace
Of Eternal Companions
Gifted by God

*With His ever-streaming
Love.*

The *World of God* is an all-embracing and ever-present Reality, accessible from within and from without, only appearing as a *hidden and far-fetched realm* to those who consider themselves realistic, practical, and of a common-sense nature, when, in fact, this most practical of all worlds lies within our God-given natures, closer than our own breath and blood.

It is the Realm of Perfections and Eternal Life, a world that forever exists, in contrast to the mind-world constructs and their temporal expressions of thoughts and feelings that traveling entities have brought and given existence to within the theater of existence.

The entities' mind-world constructs and feelings, as a collective or as individuals' expressions in a world of time, have generally become separate from the *One World* of the Creator. Lacking a common denominator, our multitudinous viewpoints result in different, often antagonistic, ways of being. Without a familiar, overarching, ideological structure to unite the gamut of variations creating and feeding the prejudices that lead to injustice and disunity, our world-consciousness becomes infected with the misconception that "my way is better than yours."

The Divine Beauty that was revealed from time immemorial, without variation or change, lacks Its expression within the collective and/or individual world-constructs. Without Its unifying assemblage and foundation, there is nothing to bind and bond the artist, the scientist, the philosopher, the spiritualist, in fact, most people to the sacredness of Life.

From the beginning that has no beginning, as the separation between our mind-world constructs and the One World of the Creator grew, and has continued to grow, causing a rift among all travelers, the resulting conditions have been aggravated, lessening the chance of survival both for our species, and for all life in general.

Without the travelers' willingness and ability to undergo a transformation that brings a Oneness of Being and Manifestation, so that we effectively integrate with our True Selves, and then manifest Their Beauty in the arena of fractional and temporal, existential experiences, travelers have triggered self-destruction.

When our worlds exist in states of separation from the One, True World of God, our worlds, individually and collectively, cannot be sustained. Our actions must derive from the God-given virtues and perfections that exemplify _a being in the station of_ the Manifestation of God, without ego or personal, selfish will; that is, through God's Grace and Mercy, we must ask to be in the State of Oneness and Manifestation, as pre-ordained by the Creator. At this level of _Understanding and Love_, all creatures "see" with His Eyes, and "hear" with His Ears.

Justice, Unity, and Peace become the natural outcome of a full integration of the Soul-based awareness (the Beauty Revealed by the Creator) with the Spirits of Life and Intelligence, and one's mind and body.

This inner functionality and clarity, at-once aligned and tuned to the Melody of Creation, reflects and expresses the Divine Plan.

Where the Light is Born

Longing
Starts from within:
The tiniest spark
Lights the star
Of enlightenment.
The Creator whispers
In our hearts
To come closer
To His inimitable, mysterious
Love.
We fall down
Like wild grass
Before the ever-Presence
Of the All-Mighty One,

Hugging the ground
As the winds of change
Blow away
Our dusty selves,
Leaving only
The sparks of Light
Glinting here—and there—
Like fireflies,
Only brighter, whiter,
Piercing the gray
Stormy days,
And new-moon nights.

It is the Love of God that brings His World from the hidden and far, Revealing His Gifts, while sustaining the traveler in a world of time. It is God's Love keeping the entity near enough to experience the Beloved of all the worlds. This Love resurrects the dead of Spirit, while quickening the blind and deaf of Soul.

It is the Love of God that gives Eternal Life—uplifting all creatures through our Remembrance of the Creator.

Eternity

Hang the Flag of Freedom
On the top-most branch
Of the Tree of Eternity
Under the Merciful Glance.

As the morning breeze blows,
Rising with the Light,
So the heart's new longing
Thrills with clear Delight.

"Here we are" for a purpose
Beyond what minds can tell:
Only our hearts hold the Secret
Dwelling beneath the swells.

As we strive towards the Mystery—
Why we live this life—
His Dream lifts us like rainbows
Beyond the cloudy strife.

Easily as the flag waves
In the winds of an Unseen Force,
So our Soul does travel
Beyond every name and form:

In the distant Joy-land,
Close within each heart,
Grow's Contentment's Garden,
Virtues flowering like art.

Asking God of His Mercy
To be brought to this land of Light,
We bask in brightest Radiance,
Surrendering to Life.

The World of God stands closer to you than your own breath, yet you know not. It is all around you, and runs through you. It is everywhere, at all times. Let your-Self see and feel it. Allow your-Self to be with your-Self.

That World is always accessible and always waiting. All it takes is one, pure desire, one moment of clarity, and—through that Divine World—signs of Nearness begin to show. The realization of Eternity's existence dawns upon you.

Everyone has a Voice, from the fifth-dimensional *vacuum* or plenum state on up. Every living and non-living, interactive participant playing a role in the ultimate composition of the Life and Intelligence of creation has a say: that expression of his or her individual existence, while also being a member of One Creation. When we ignore this fundamental level of communication, this right to coexist, anywhere and everywhere, we violate the sacredness of an existence that is God-given.

Those who ignore the Creator's Plan interfere with, and/or block, the Intended Purpose of His Creation. His Love expresses It-Self throughout Domains that become unreachable and uninhabited by those that interfere and destroy Life. For those that understand and practice the Eternal Wisdom of *Surrender and Submission* to His Will and Pleasure, the Door is always open to the Revealed Beauty and Blessings of His Creation.

This right to Self-expression and the concurrent obligation to follow the Creator's Plan are applicable to all forms of Life. The planet Earth is obliged to give shelter and resources. To all life living upon it. Members of the mineral, plant, and animal Kingdoms through their Spirits of Life and Intelligence (minerals use attraction and repulsion, plants using growth, and animals using instinctive intelligence) fulfill their obligations to the Whole of Life. Yet, despite the fact that we Soul-possessing humans have been given the greatest <u>potential capacity</u> for correct and virtuous behavior, along with greater responsibility for protecting and caring for all of life, we have failed to be the <u>good stewards</u> of life that we were meant to be

The result is that entities who have traveled to Earth through their Soul-based point of view find that this long-standing and purposeful ignoring of the rights of various members of Life, caused by those entities known as human, through their insatiable, greedy appetite for material things and temporal power, has brought everyone and everything upon this planet to the brink of extinction, again!

Is it fair to say that the warnings of God's Emissaries have fallen on deaf ears? Time-and-again, have we not persecuted, tortured, and killed these Divine Educators as a convenience, and as a sign of arrogance, resisting and ignoring the warnings of our Creator?

Both individually and collectively, we cannot continue to ignore all the signs of an impending catastrophe. We must face eons of violations of the sacredness of Life on the Planet, our home. We must humbly invite in God's Love and Wisdom to transform our minds and hearts, and thereby have the possibility—through Divine Super-positioning according to God's Will and Pleasure—of avoiding a calamity whose signs, and whose causes, we are blind to.

Without the Love from the Creator, we appear doomed. Without a quick solution to the myriad issues facing us, we will be unable to continue living as a species, along with the Whole of Life, on, and including, our precious planet Earth.

The language of the *Heart of it All* appears to be saying that a critical time has come to turn to God, the Creator. Not a minute too late, the Call has been given to Remember and Return. The conditions and circumstances loudly proclaim,

"Here I am, Lord." Let us turn in repentance and change our ways!

In gratitude to my mother....

Letting Go

Happiness comes from within—
It cannot be measured in things.
All the gold in all the worlds
Vanishes when eternity springs.

The welling up of Joy,
Letting go of sorrows,
Is God's way, the Soul's path,
Bringing ever-tomorrows.

Beyond the mind's cognizance
All Understanding comes,
God's purview being each
entity's Good:
Each Being's Truth follows.

Long for the Day when
the light shines least
On the dusty mortal trail,
For then shines the Soul's
Noon-bright Sun
Spreading Light that never fails.

The Next World is purely bright;
Finding God within is allowed—
Ordained—there
Upon the Branch of Love,
Where the eagle's might
Is claimed.

The Garden

The watchman brings Souls
To Eternity's gate:
Where Mercy cradles hearts—
Nudges fate.

His most tender Touch
Bows us down like rainbows,
Our in-most Beings bright
With multicolored splendor.

The scent of roses nearby,
The river splashing a refrain,
Why not bask in God's Garden
Where Glory remains?

Feel the lightness of your feet
As you breathe in the Mystery.
This New Land welcomes all
Like a Heart-beat beyond history.

All the leaves on every tree
Stay thankful for His Grace
As we move beneath the branches,
Each Self rooted in place.

To realize that Self-awareness, and that, as an observer. one's "I-ness" or Soul experiences that which exists from within and from without, always, is an effect and reflection of a Creator that is forever Self-aware, Being the Eternal One that Observes— that is *Enlightenment*.

Out of Nothingness

Each _Unknowable Essence_—the creature is My Mystery, and I am his or her Mystery—comes to existence through the Soul that mirrors forth its infinite potential in transit and transcendence, out of a _Desire to be Known and to Know, to be Loved and to Love_. As designed by the Creator, this _Self-aware Being of Light_ emerges as _a point of entry or gate_ that splits the Sea of Nothingness at its event horizon.

Polarity is now born in the form of two "wells:" a loving, Soul-based awareness and a "mound" of conscious intellect. Imagine yourself at the beach digging a hole in the sand. This hole or _well_ represents the spiritual heart being continuously filled with Soul-based Love and Divine Knowledge. The mound, or up-side-down _well_, formed from the sand scooped out of the hole, symbolizes the intellect ever-filling with mental constructs from physiologically-based, sense-perceived understandings.

This process occurs through the modulations on two, bi-directional scalar waves. The first, non-linear (time-wise) wave arises from the Soul's tenth-dimensional Source. The second, linear (time-wise) wave begins from the fifth-dimensional, vacuum or plenum state, at the quantum and sub-quantum levels—the Spirits in the Universe. Here energy, first as a potential, and then expressed as action (what energy "is" and what energy "does"), becomes a force, that through the fourth-dimensional chamber of creativity, manifests the pairing phenomenon in human companionships, and, time-forward, allows for the Beauty of life, love, and rational intelligence. Forming the entity's "I-ness," this Divine directive gives the Soul-possessing Being the ability to think, feel, and reflect, allowing the individual to translate and transform, deep within, as well as without (epigenetically), at the square root of the speed of light.

A membrane rises into existence at the point of entry of Soul-based awareness, giving birth to the string connecting the two "wells," and from within and from without, emerges a universe, a plenum out of the split and pairing of wells of nothingness!

A trans-dimensional Soul embarks on a journey of separation from its Source, as a Spirit of Life and Intelligence, a force disguised as an imperceptible field of activities, attracting and repulsing, growing into view, acquiring consciousness and sense perception of an environ all around, emerging into a rational being, stretching and grasping the Unknown, wrapped by an inner force of Faith, a transcendent confidence that begs for a Return to Source.

The nothingness has become something, as observers of a forming actuality, and as reflective entities that begin to understand the purpose of their inner immersion and emergence into the shores of consciousness. There is then meaning and direction!

The dot of Light and point of entry, an observing Being, switches the point of view as a participant into a line, and elsewhere a string appears, looking forwards and backwards in time. In a realm of names and appearances, the entity lives a fractional and temporal experience, and reflecting upon his or her existence, *evolves in Knowingness and Lovingness*.

The Well of Love

The longing for God's Love
Is filled in an easy way:
One opens one's Heart
And asks.
The fulfillment of Love
Is experienced in this way:
One acts from one's Heart
And Soul.
All the longing and desires
Of this world are answered
When God pours His Love
Into the humble recipient's Heart.
Like a well ever-filling,
The Heart brims with

Happiness,
Joy,
Contentment.
Relax into this Love.
All the answers to Life are there,
Easy to obtain
As drinking a cup of water
Filled at the never-ending
Spring.

Close Within

The Soul's castle Is vast and wide,
Holding an Ocean brimming
with Wisdom
--His Love.
Dive within to find
Everything you need:
A ship of Life
To sail eternal Realms,

The Breeze of God's Mercy
To carry you
Wherever you need to go,
Endless Waters floating you
Nearer
To the Mysterious Essence
Just over the horizon.

Of course, you'll find your-Self
Soon sitting next to the One
Meant just for you—
Two people's hands
Holding the tiller
As God's Breath
Fills the sails,
Washes your faces,
So that you laugh together
At how easily the Infinite Delight
Spreads.

Within each Adamic Cycle come numerous Dispensations of Divine Information—Disclosures of the Divine Will and Pleasure—assessing Spiritual Development against Their own Standard, accompanied by the purifying *Fire* of detachment and change.

These transformative processes address and challenge all concurrent knowledge and practices, bringing about an apocalypse or removal of the veils of ignorance and mismanaged passions interposed between the creature and the Creator. Outwardly, this transformative purification and cleansing appears as a destructive force associated with the pain and suffering of resistance, customs, conduct and practices contrary to His Will and Pleasure. Inwardly, the process of purification and cleansing renews and reorients the creatures' understandings and hearts towards their True Purpose, and, the significance of their fractional and temporal, existential experiences.

These phenomena have repeated Themselves on our planet at least one thousand times, each lasting fifty thousand years. These events have all highlighted a Standard representing a little over seven percent of the Divine Objective, reminding the creatures of their True Station, in Remembrance of The Lord of all the worlds—their Return.

Around the middle of the eighteen hundreds, _a New Revelation_ of the Divine Dispensation was delivered, fueling the creatures' Spiritual transformation, and bringing the completion of the Spiritual Criterion, the required _Divine Touchstone_ signaling both our further progressive, Spiritual evolution, and the Creator's Final Purpose for humanity—a five-hundred thousand-year cycle of development. The turmoil and apocalyptic process removing the veils of ignorance and mismanaged passions can be today witnessed.

Despite its painful appearance and actuality, this process of purification is a good thing, a Blessing prophesied during the many Adamic Cycles gone by. God's Will and Pleasure shall be done on Earth as it is done in Heaven.

Every Divine Reckoning, or Judgment, during a Day of God—a period following the Divine Dispensation—represents a necessary adjustment or correction to all human endeavor towards Self, and, collectively, towards a common Goal lying beyond the survival of the species—the Remembrance and Return to the Creator.

However tense and confusing the shedding of the heart's impurities may be, as well as obtaining the clarity of mind required to do the right thing always, the species is, once again, being guided towards the realization that the Creator is in charge, and this is a designed Divine Plan that knows no beginning.

The more we resist, ignore, disbelieve, or refute His Plan, the harder and longer the Spiritual, transformative process will be. This Highest Standard will supplant, and be superposed upon, the brow and heart of all His creatures!

The Land of Rainbows

Beyond the light we see
Disappearing at Earth's horizon
Is the Light of the un-dying
Realm lighting each heart
With the Fire
Of God's Love.
O lift us up, dear Lord,
Beyond our petty concerns
About coins of the country,
Or the body's humble needs.
From the other side, Thy Kingdom,
A Nightingale's trill permeates
With the sound of a mountain stream
Rushing swift and clear
Over the cliff,
Collapsing in colors,
Filling an endless Day.

Eternal Life

What does it feel like
In the Land of Light,
Where Eternity flows
Like a River of Joy?
The heart is blessed with happiness,
Blossoming perfectly—
No petals falling.

What does it sound like
In the Ever-flowing Land?
The clearest, sweetest
Spring-song
Brushes across the Soul's ear,
The Heart's listening.

What does it smell like
In the meadows
Of fresh and abundant
Wildflowers?

The most tantalizing sweet scents
Beyond mortal imaginings
Fill the Inner Being
With delight.

How do the days pass
Where the Sun of Truth
Shines brilliantly
Without blinding—
Lighting up Life's Presence
With the Wisdom of Ages?
Each Eternal Being bows within
To the Rays of God's Mercy,
Knowing itself as nothing,
And knowing the Invisible
One as Ever-present,
All-powerful,
Embracing every Living Thing
In a Love
Beyond measure.

Oneness

There is a River of Love
Flowing through each Heart
Sent by God
To animate each of His creatures.
Rejoice in the Knowingness
That each of us shares:
That every River
Flows into His Ocean
Of Understanding;
Each Soul is lit
With the Inner Radiance
To sustain infinite lifetimes
Until—time beyond time—
The moment comes
For that Bright Being
To sally forth and land
On Eternal shores....

Thanks be to God
Who decides
In an instant of Grace
That mortal lives are done
And the Life close to Him
Has—seemingly—begun,
Though we always were,
Not of Earth, born of Heaven,
And have been,
Seated in the green grass
Beneath His favorite Tree,
Listening to Him speak
About Love, sharing, and caring,
Turning every dream
Of Eternity
Into the celestial-colored wildflowers
We gently touch.

Disappearance

Within the heart of the Ruby
Is a Light that shines forever.
Surround your-Self with
this crystal cave
To reflect God's Way of Splendor.
Nothing can be lost
That's contained and protected
In this red Ark of Eternal Truth.

Discover the Ship of Self
Sailing before the winds of longing
Until it disappears
Beneath the bright, illumining
Golden Rays.
Of the Infinite Sun.

Contemplating on our inner silence, we hear the
only Voice that matters—the Lord of all the worlds.

The need to be careful, as we voice our opinions to others, then becomes apparent, for we all are being heard by the All-seeing Lord. This ultimate state of awareness brings to the traveling entity the needed repose, and tranquility of mind and heart, amidst an Ocean of harmonious balance permeating Creation.

The Lord reveals: through your silence, you hear Me. Through your tranquility, you feel My Presence. Through your humble countenance, you know I Am here. Through your service, you experience the nobility of My Creation.

Us and Them

From time immemorial, all traveling entities have mistakenly learned to assign one of two categories to those beings we are familiar with. Those we perceive as friendly, acceptable, and complementary are designated as **_us_** (e.g. "He or she is one of us"), and are given special treatment of a positive nature.

The "others," viewed as opposites, are perceived to be unfriendly, unacceptable and antagonistic. Consequently, the latter entities are mentally shoved into virtual oblivion, by being termed **_them_**.

To justify this polarization and emphasize the contrast, travelers have used any and all reasons possible, some easier to understand, and others lacking logic and common sense. This divisive *__mind-set__* affects the way each entity *__feels__* about other entities (as well as his or her Self-conception and Self-love). Thus, the traveler's heart becomes preferentially set one way or the other, destroying the Unity of the species through this pre-conceived, false understanding of relationships.

Familiarity, as in family, can give access and rapport among the membership. On the other hand, family relationships where one or more members are abused (physically, mentally, emotionally, or spiritually) leads to profound divisions affecting the very bedrock of human civilization.

This primal coloring of the traveler's heart and mind often lasts throughout his or her sojourn in a world of time. Only in extreme circumstances is the traveler able to sever and reverse such an early environmental modulation, and mentally to move another human being from the column of them to the column of _**us**_—changing the perception of another Being of Light from that of an unfriendly individual—even an enemy—to that of a welcome friend.

This special conditioning and/or indoctrination has migrated from the family to other associations or groups such as the military, political parties, religious associations, etc., where the concept of _brother- and sister- hood_ go beyond blood lines. Here, too, the terms "us" and "them" carry strong meanings—one influencing the conditions of physical life and death.

Love's Answer

Here's the question:
Do you want to know
How you were created?
What is it you are made of?
When did your existence begin?
The answer lies within.
Dive through
The Heart's Knowingness
To the Source of All.
You are one of many sparks
Lit by your Creator
In the beginning
That has no beginning.
You were born
As a Soul-possessing entity
Because God wished
To Know of Him-Self
In the Form of the "Other,"
Through Love.

Love is the linkage,
The invisible, binding force
Uniting all.
Without the Creator's
Love—for Himself,
Our love for Him,
His Love for us,
There would be no creation.
So rejoice
In the variety of life—
Each precious
Mineral, plant, animal,
Human, extra-terrestrial being
Exists, blossoms,
As an emanation of Love.
Love is the basis of all,
The reason for all,
And the purpose of all.
Love, alone,
Gives life a purpose.
Ya Baha'ul'abha.

Re-birth

When the world was young
And humans were innocent,
When the animals and plants
Had no fear,
When the sky was clear blue
Or raining crystal tears,
And the oceans surged
In one melody of Love,
While the mountain streams
Slipped past green mosses
And small, sandy inlets—
Or roared by rocky
Embankments—
Then we knew the Friend.
Hand-in-hand
With our Creator's
Blessed and Manifested
Form, our hearts blossomed
Like the first roses to open

Their delicate, pink petals
In spring,
With a scent so lovely
The angels bent down
To imbibe it.
"Why not now?"
You may ask—
And you would be right.
For in God's World
There is neither time,
Nor decay.
Place your-Self there,
In your secret
Heart-of-Hearts,
And "there" becomes "here."
Again, Eden is born
Without sin, and Love
Whispers its infinite names
Wherever you turn
In this
Most blessed,

Cherished, Perfectly-loved, Sweetly-enfolded Realm.

What is of interest is the obvious fact that in Reality we are all supposed to be a part of the first column—the "_**us**_" aspect, whether friendly or not, welcomed or to be avoided at all costs. There are no justifications that allow or excuse any behavior in violation of the _Standard_ set by God's Representatives. The moment that we excuse, accept under special circumstances, ignore or promote, participate or engage in behavior deemed inappropriate, and in violation of the rules conditioning the whole of society, we are no longer victims of the problems of society; we are their source and cause.

In fact, all bets are off.

These violations are symptomatic of a deeper issue residing at the core of evil: the denial of God's existence, and God's All-Seeing Eye. Whether we are ignorant of the Truth, or unwilling to acknowledge it, the results are the same. A heart that is empty of the Love of God will be filled by whatever else is around.

Just because the traveler is blind and deaf of Spirit, and disconnected from his or her Soul, is not a justification or excuse for becoming the evil that acts as source and cause of all that is not good or of benefit to Self, family, community, state, nation, and the world.

The continuing promotion of hatred and division has only inflamed the world's condition. Entities have increased in iniquity, acting from hearts filled with malice and lies, using deceptive techniques to corral and direct public opinion, and painting images that obfuscate the truth that would otherwise have taken "*us*" in another direction.

The resulting danger is obvious. Just like life is coming to an end everywhere, our species may soon cease to be a member of this Earthly environ. Concurrently, concepts that bring "*us*" together, that foster unity and justice, are disappearing into oblivion, hardly used and remembered, while a new generation is being conditioned and indoctrinated by these violently separating descriptions and definitions that do not allow for discussion and/or an agreement to disagree.

The latter moderate stand would give "*us*" the time, the tolerance and the acceptance of "*our*" differences of opinion and understanding, allowing for the individual right, and the freedom to change our minds, to amicably look forward, as citizens of the world, to improvements we all have agreed are crucial and necessary to focus our attention upon. The consequential Unity would serve as the basis for our willingness to carry on, without the distractions and fear of belonging to any one column—since either one is the wrong one for someone else.

The Living Jewel

Pray to break the loop of
unknowingness.
Pray to be released from wrong.
Pray for the Balm for
the unhealed heart,
To hear the Celestial Song.

Hearken to the Whispers
of the Voice within.
Listen to the Maestro's baton
Guiding all His servants
to the pathless Path,
Stemming cries from the
beleaguered throng.

Dawn is near for those who long
For His inestimable Presence:
A shining Star alighting
on the Heart—
Nowhere is His Light more present.

Finally, two have merged,
The timeless with the time,
Leaving just a string of mortal life.
The thread of "me" rewinds to Self—
Eternity lifting eagle-like.

Far from an eternal companionship, the traveler seeks for one that will give him or her a life-time partnership. Yet, time-and-again, this is measured, at best, in years.

The illusory strength of the "***us and them***" continues to play a role and influence, a pattern determined stubbornly to stand its ground, day-after-day, against those caught-up in its snare.

The effects of this inner evil, the sounds of whose beating drum have assaulted our very being across millennia with their waves of destruction, can only be overcome through the intercession of the All-Powerful One—as we surrender our Soul to the Mystic Melody of Divine Unity.

The Connection

This journey of life
Is a trail of tears—
Nothing lasts.
All turns to dust.
The spinning star of the Soul
Can transform it.
Let it.
Allow the Ocean of Knowingness
To sweep across the sands
Of mortal lives.
Receive the Full Moon's
Perfect reflection—
Illuminating the Truth
Of God's ever-present
Love.
No one is left behind,
Ever.
Deep within bubbles the spring
Of "Here I am, Lord."

Let it loose in grateful prayer.
His Gaze, His Smile,
Will embrace thy-Self
In Joy.

Closer

At each point in the universe
A new Reality begins,
Leading always to God—
The All-Knowing, the All-Wise.
How to find the right point
To take you there quickest?
Go within and listen
For the Voice.
Go without and find the One
Who encompasses Every Point
In every hidden Word.
There is no greater Secret
Than this: marking time

By where you are
On the Spiral Journey
Into the Immortal
Realm.
Heart-felt Knowingness
Lights up the Path
On the pathless-journey
For at His Command
The endless traveler
Arrives.

It was all a dream
Within the Mind of God
That ends
Where it started—
In a big bang
Of bliss—a kiss
From the All-Merciful
Who Loves each of His creatures
Despite their hesitations,
Little bumps and hiccups,

On the endless road
To perfection—the Presence
Of the One.

Oneness

The light at the end of the tunnel
Is closer than you think—
It lies within thy heart,
Thy Soul's dwelling place.
There is no reason to despair
At the trials and tribulations
Of the world,
The evil deeds of men.
The Light within glows
Within each of them—
It can never be extinguished.
Without a doubt
The clouds of iniquity
Can easily be blown away

By the tiniest Breath of Truth
Sent through the Word
Of the Almighty Unifier.
There is not one entity
Who has not been birthed
Through the Creative Will
Of God. All
Creatures will return
Unto their All-Merciful Creator.
Though the minds of humans
Are filled with the obscuring
Dust of divisive and hateful
Thoughts, they may be
Washed clean by the All-
Encompassing Love
Of the Divine Being.
Oneness is the Reality.
Separation is the illusion.
The sun-filled sky
Always returns
After the rains.

Rejoice in the ever-lasting
Wonderment,
Astonishment,
At the gifts He bestows
Upon each one of us,
And revel in the Light
That will shine forth
At His decree
And His behest.
There is no other Light
But the Light
Of the One True God,
Who unites all
In His infinite, mysterious
Brilliance.

Observe how languages, traditions, cultures, gender and sexual inclinations, roles and scripts, and belief systems, have been made to augment and perpetuate any distinction supporting the "*us*" and "_**them**_" mentality. Notice how idiomatic expressions, arising from hearts filled with hate and anger, have led to violently-expressed dissatisfaction arising from these entities' egoic selves. In the end, these waves of destructive forces have materialized as seeds that grow and multiply, bringing about the poisonous fruits that offer many appearances, yet share two symptoms throughout—ignorance and mismanaged passions.

Central to the theme of a godless societal order, we find intolerance, violence, disorder, mental and physical illnesses, and environmental cross-contamination causing inhospitable Earth-based conditions, prejudice of all sorts, greed, jealousy, and envy. The Love of God bringing us and everything together—a functioning planetary system of Life and Intelligence—in contrast, is self-evident.

The Love of God is a unifying and integrating, omni-dimensional, and multi-directional force. At the core of existence, It is what brings Life into creation, sustaining and brings relationships into blossoming eternally.

Emotional expressions without the Divine Love divide and separate. God's Love must permeate throughout Life, feeding the expanse of Soul, Spirit, mind, and body; harmonizing all families, and permanently bonding all entities as it reflects the eternal in a temporal actuality. It is the Love of God that builds everything, an Eternal in a temporal attraction that endures and acts, even in life-after-life.

An Ocean of Carrier Waves

Deep within the "vacuum"—a plenum only appearing to be empty space—unmanifested existence coalesces into an entangled, quantum chaos, from which state it expresses its innate Beauty, to be observed and interacted with by journeying, Soul-possessing entities, as the completion of a universe, one of many, begins.

Dots of Light emerge, eventually phase-conjugating into stand-alone, uninterrupted, bi-directional, linearly-expressed carrier waves—gravitationally forming, biologically structuring, and electromagnetically operating their units of transport. Such a process occurs when the entity's Soul integrates at conception with a physical form. Entities' Soul-possessing states of pure awareness find themselves encased as prisoners in temporal bodies—making them the perfect audience for the Simulator's theater of fractional and temporal, existential experiences, the Sojourn.

Each traveler is given a role and a script, within a matrix conditioned by differing cultures, rites and beliefs, languages, education, genetics, and the environment. The information given and acquired is most likely incomplete or manipulated by others, with earlier travelers competing for control of the local assets that ensure a better quality of survival.

As observers and participants interact within a theater of possibilities, many agendas emerge. The resulting fabric of actuality is layered and embedded, consisting of superposed, modulated carrier waves influencing our lives the way a production team adds layers of seeming reality to an action film. This System of Life and Intelligence runs continually as civilizations, names, and appearances rise-and-fall, reflecting the illusory dreams and nightmares of populations on planets in solar systems, galaxies, and universes, near-and-far.

Perhaps the film is paused to focus on one life— your life. In that moment, your Soul-based awareness becomes clarified in God's Great Scheme. Then the film advances, scene-after-scene rolling over time, showing the movement of all life, patterns emerging as history, advancing all creation towards Divine Perfection.

The Blessing

My Love reaches the horizon
Of the infinite, Solar realms.
My Love enters the Mystery
Of the inner Rose of Peace.

My Love extends beyond thinking
To where the Heart knows Light,
For wherever My Love shines forth,
Thy destiny shines bright.

No stone of mere fortune
Can withstand the sweeping away—
My Love's breath draws all Souls close,
Surrendered as they pray.

My Love only knows Mercy,
Each creature being My Trust.
To trust in Me is thy highest good—
To fall to My Love is best.

Happy is the one who, united,
Sees My Love everywhere.
Strife is gone, oneness abides,
In a world where Love repairs.

Let My Love be thy calling card,
Banishing all despair.
My Love shines like a million suns:
My Reign of Light prevails.

Here

In the meadows of springtime,
In the green and sere woods,
God breathes upon each creature,
All doing what they should.

You and I go walking, talking,
As angels smile from above,
In this Paradise brought near—here—
Overflowing with Love.

The Creator's Grace descends,
Gently watering every Soul,
The Tree of Blessing and rising Peace,
O'er shadows to make us whole.

The Holy and inimitable One
Bestows upon us all
A golden ocean of foaming waves
Bringing Word from distant shores.

Entering the Beyond

Along the narrow road to eternity,
Signs of Oneness appear
along the way:
Here a friendship healed,
a bond restored;
There a sorrowful heart mended
With the invisible Breeze of Love.

When the path feels long,
Thirst almost unbearable,
The Lord of all
Slips around the corner
Like a suddenly-appearing Friend
To offer a cool glass of clear water.
"Don't worry," He says.
"There's plenty more where that
Came from."

Walking, you come upon a white,
Wrought-iron gate,
Pleasingly shaped into curving
Vines and flowers.
It opens at a touch
Onto a meadow of wildflowers
Blooming.

A Luminous Figure beckons you
With a smile.
Many celestial beings are seated

Around festive tables
Adorned with food and drink.
"Welcome. Welcome. Join the party,"
They say.

Your eternal companion approaches,
Eyes shining, saying,
"I've saved you a seat."
Seated together at the
round, white table
Both of you look up
At the perfect sky, listen
To mysterious, infinite, varied
Songs of birds among lush foliage,
Grateful
Beyond words.

Rise and Let Go

Gaze at a rainbow
And you'll observe
How the colors effervesce
Into white
Light.
Just so our Selves
Merge in the Unity
Of God's Grace—
A Oneness
Of Purpose and Intent.

How long has it been
Since we remembered
That we light up
The same sky
From the same Soul's
Sunlight,
Moon-beams?
There is no separation when

Our hearts are one
In the point
And line
Of Eternity.

Find within
That land
Where the ocean of everyone
Meets the shoreline of the Self,
Gently surrendering to the Divine
Like a wave rising,
Descending, water
Particles sinking invisibly
Into the sand.

In the midst of it all, the eternal questions surface:

Who am I? Why am I here? Where did I come from?

Where am I going?

The Spirit or force of Faith stands as the means

to answer these questions. We must find the belief in one's Self, and beyond that, with conviction and assurance, a belief in, and relationship with, one's Creator—as Manifested.

The Manifestations of God are the Source for us of the Creator's Love and Eternal Life—embrace Them as you embrace your own life.

Enlightenment

Is nothing more
Than the whisper of God's
Grace each early
Morning
Bringing the Sun to
Light-up
The heart.
Such anticipation
Fills us

Each time we
Awaken
To radiate
The endless Day
With gratitude, swimming
In Joy.

Constructs and Feelings

There are two Realms: one within the Simulator and Trainer, and the other outside. The first represents _creation_ as we experience it. Here causes and effects come and go. Worlds-upon-worlds exist as contingent systems of life and intelligence, where causality, destiny and fate, from within and from without, are the conditions through which we time-travelers move forward.

The second one speaks of a Realm of Revelations that has always existed, that knows neither beginning nor end. It is _not_ a domain of causality, karma, and connections as we think of them within our Simulation of Life and Intelligence.

Here in the first realm we coalesce two types of understanding.

One is derived from the material world, and the other from the Spirit that permeates the All.

The resulting understanding, our state of knowingness at any given moment, is always changing as we are being modulated from within and from without: through our genetics, the environment, our egoic self, and from our Soul-based awareness and Spiritual heart.

Everyone everywhere in creation undergoes this ever-changing realization of her or his understanding as an effect and its expression: the *life we live and experience*.

Each mind-world construct exists in its own space-and-time track as each entity emerges into this planetary System of Life and Intelligence. Each individual, as a bubble of knowingness, coexists linearly, time-wise, with others, interacting and exchanging thoughts and feelings, influencing and being influenced.

Despite the enormity of our world, an individual linearly interacts with relatively few other entities, creating relationships as families and communities grow. What is of interest is that, at any given moment, in whatever time frame this phenomenon is addressed, all of these interacting worlds of coalesced understanding coexist individually, having only some aspects of their constructs shared. There are many more diverse and different understandings underpinning how we each live and experience what we think of as *reality*.

What any individual understands and believes his or her existence to be is never exactly the same as anyone else's belief. Whatever the small percentage of similarities that can be shared, there is always a greater amount of dissimilar aspects among mind-world constructs. Our opinions and life-styles speak of this omni-dimensional and multi-directional arrangement, its patterns, and the collective message carried as a civilization.

The fabric of this collective reality is either advancing successfully, or it is not. For the most part, our collective effort has demonstrated a repetitive pattern of self-destruction, and with it, a parallel effect on the environment shared as it, too, vanishes over time.

What this tells us is that our coalesced understandings *have always been wrong*. The proper realization emerging from our feelings, thoughts, words, and actions, one that results in unity and oneness, has never taken root insofar as the fabric of the actuality shared by all the members, grouped as a collective that represents our species in the here-and-now.

When we look at this phenomenon from the point of view of individuals, or the whole, we understand that the pattern and message is the same. What we each think, believe, speak of, and act upon, runs against the realization of that which endures and sustains life everywhere and always. Whatever we understand is not providing the ingredients to produce lives filled with either happiness and clarity of mind or relationships modulated by the continuing effects of a Divine Life as the Source of the oneness and unity that continually manifests an actuality mirroring the Eternal Domain of its Creator, as designed—the fabric of the Kingdom of God.

A Conversation

This loss of life,
these confusions,
in a God-less world,
are a gain for other
worlds. These Souls
will keep growing.
Who knows what lesson

each entity must learn—
or the world as a whole?
We are all here on our
own journeys—to lean
closer-and-closer
to our Creator's Heart,
as bamboo leans in a storm
towards the sheltering cave.

Still, so many children dying
and we ask, as servants,
"Is it necessary?"
An answer comes:
"<u>There is not a moment
to lose.</u>
Upheavals everywhere
are shaking up the soil
of human hearts
so the new Love may
be planted."

"How may we help?"

"Do not lose hope. All
that is winnowed here
is replanted somewhere else.
Tend to the soil
Of your own heart.
Let the rest be.
See how the sun rises
each morning and sets
each evening. Let
the rhythm of nature
guide thy life. Rise
each day with new
determination to live
the life God's Representatives
have lived. Work
For the good of the whole.
Never let the ego
overrule thy higher
knowingness.

Follow the flight,
instead, of the golden
Eagle—the swift
and sure gliding
one.
Let My Pleasure be
thy ruling command.
Good luck and blessings.
I will see you
on the other side."

I bow in my mind and
heart—reassured.
"This too shall pass."
Let us take courage
and use each rising
day to the best advantage
for all life everywhere.

Thus, if you Love, so will your journey be filled
with life and blessings.

Uplifted

Enlightenment is nothing
Save the lifting-up of the Soul
To heights unimaginable.
The human entity was destined
By God to exhibit the traits
And conditions of immortality.

Instead we have fallen
To the lowest levels of depravity,
Sunk below the instinctive animal,
Or the plant, growing towards the sun,
Groveling in the dirt
Less steadfast than the rock.

What has become of the noble
Creature fashioned by the All-
Mighty?
Where have Soul and Spirit fled,
Leaving behind the empty, lonely

Physical form?
Why do the cries of millions of lost
Souls not reach the All-Knowing
One's hearing?

What can we do to reverse
This trend of humans
Running from their Maker?
They are unwilling to see or hear from
The Person of His Glory,
Who has arrived in the Holy land,
In the pre-ordained time,
Establishing
The Rule of Pen Over sword,
Peace Over war,
And over endless divisions—
Unity.

We pledge our-Selves
To serve the Divine Pleasure
In whatever way is necessary

That the species known
As human may be lifted up—
Again—as of old
To the heights of
understanding, knowing
That there is no God but He,
The One,
Indivisible and Merciful
Patron of all life
Everywhere.

Spiraling Up

One way, and one way only
Leads to the Immortal Life:
Beyond strife and discord
Is the way of the Lord's
Will that fills the Soul
With Joy.

Who can question
What is right
Determined by the Infinite
Mind—and rained down
From the Heaven
Of the Creator's
Infinite possibilities?

Why not follow God's lead
So as not to miss
The intersection
Of the way of Right Action
With the highway of desire?

Sometimes it's hard to let go
Of small happiness
Only to find an empty road
And yet, suddenly a
gentle rain descends.
The desert's soon populated
With every sort of creature

Shouting from Joy
As the Envoy of Love
Appears, bringing a New Spring,
Clothed in the effervescent, rainbow
Garment of Perfection.

The Land of Love

Beyond the water's edge,
In the middle of the sea,
Where the lights of distant shores
Cannot reach Heart's sensibility,

The Inner Light finds its way,
Lighting each Soul's Beacon,
Guiding us aright, as we
Sail and land—
As only He can.

Beyond the faintest thought,
In the Paradise of the First Mind,
Is the Knowingness of One
Who all the chains unbinds!

Let loose the joy and sorrow.
Regain the strength of peace.
In the world of no tomorrows
Lies the ever-present "we."

Oneness of Soul, Affection
and Mercy,
Here Love overflows;
Each being rejoices for all the virtues
That God's Love bestows.

This Day thus is full of Beauty.
A soothing light enfolds each pair.
You and I will soon be embracing
The One Love that's always shared.

Rejoice

Beyond the last buoy,
Past the horizon's edge,
Where the dawning light
Shows pink and bright
Above the city's edge,
The Lord of All is waiting,
With a smile broad as time
For each creature born
Of Eternal Love
To unite each heart
With Thine.
Thankfulness and glory!
Celebrate the Infinite One
Who Mercifully invites us
To the Holy Kingdom come.

Time-less

Let each creature preform
His or her mission in the allotted
Time.
For while time advances,
The Eternal One remains
The same, watching
Each being advance
On the evolutionary journey
Towards the endless Oneness
Of All Life
Everywhere.
For the Message
From the Messengers
Is that God waits for no one,
While the Eternal King
Yet receives His servants
As they come knocking at the Door,
In time-less time.

Waves of Love: A Song for Children

First, we love God,
Then receive His Love—
Riding on the waves of Holy Spirit.
We spread That Love around
On the planet and above,
Swimming in the waves
Of Holy Spirit.
Sharing kindness and Joy,
Giving ourselves a hug,
From our hearts so pure and strong
With the Love that overflows
From our Most Beloved,
On the waves of the Holy Spirit.

Without the Will and Pleasure of God overseeing the life of each human being, the mortal life is useless. The infinite time-track is only superimposed according to the dictates of the Almighty One. Without His Blessings, our mortal lives are trapped by the circumstances of time and space through the machinations of our egoic modulations—small self-conditioning.

Therefore, we must strive our utmost to obey the dictates of the Supreme Commander, in order to reach that heavenly state where the Soul is free to experience what our Creator wishes for us, rather than what we personally think that we need.

Message for the Children and Young People

Let the light of God's Love
fill your hearts.
Let the Unity of God's
Messengers fill your minds.

Allow your hearts to overflow
with the endless blessings
Of the One Who is a Mystery
to all creatures.
Let the dawn of a New Day arise
In the Country of God's
kind of freedom:
Following the Creator's Will,
You will be led to fly
Like an eagle in Heaven.
Thankful,
Prayerful,
Delighting in the gifts
Of God's creation,
We are ready servants to the Lord.

At each point in our journeys to enlightenment, our Souls expand into the Oneness of Knowledge and Wisdom given by the Lord of All Knowledge and Wisdom. This process is like a crystal that is continuously honed and turned within the waves of the Divine Breath, until it is the perfect shape to be played like a tuning fork with the touch of the Divine Hand.

Each time an experience in life confirms the unity and oneness of us all, and our total dependency upon the Divine Creator, the crystal-sounding quality and perfection of our Soul is increased until we are each a perfect whole—truly aligned with, and obedient to, the awesome, all-powerful Will and Pleasure of the Creator through His latest Manifestation.

Any gratefulness and gratitude that we may exhibit in our spiritual hearts can never come close to the depth of gratitude that in Reality would be needed to be a proper degree of thankfulness to the All-powerful Being ruling the lives of each and every creature.

It is only through God's merciful intervention in our poor, meek lives that we are even able to exist—potentially growing into the Beautiful Beings of Light and Kindness that we were always meant to be.

Life for each one of us is a gift that we were given in order to experience the ultimate freedom that this dependence on God has gifted us. Without this Light of Divine Guidance, we wander through dark nights, floating on stormy seas, always about to collide with any number of destructive obstacles to our spiritual growth, or to capsize our tiny boats in seas of unmeasured depths. Without the Divine Admiral of our unworthy vessels, we would soon perish in the tempestuous temptations of egoic lusts, and nameless fears. With our steady and steadfast Guide, we can allow the winds of Divine Destiny to carry us without effort to the Shoreless Lands, where the Sun of Truth stands waiting for each of us with open arms, and an infinitely-understanding Heart.

The Way to Go

Along the path to righteousness,
Past the abyss of ego,
The Soul is strengthened
By loving wisdom—
Boundless as the sea goes.

Far beyond mere Knowingness,
Past the horizon of horizons,
The heart breathes in
Pure lovingness, following
Where He Chose.

We cannot find the way ourselves.
We follow the Beacon bright!
For even the sharpest-sighted traveler,
Cannot discern in night.

Follow the path to freedom,
Where only the Soul alights,
And every Being shines like a star
Pointing to Beauty's Might.

If you chance to ask directions,
Make sure Whom you ask is True,
A Righteous Being Come from God
Whose actions follow through.

There is nowhere to go.
There is nowhere to turn,
Except the Point of Unity
Blessing more than we've earned.

A Conversation

In the middle of the ocean
The Soul cries out
For guidance.
"Help me, dear Lord,"

She asks, "for without you
I cannot find my way to the shore."
"I am here—near,"
The Lord's Messenger,
The Glory of all Glories,
Replies.
"Draw me closer,"
The surrendered Soul asks.
The Lord has pity
And stretches out a hand
Like a bolt of lightning,
Illumining the dark waters
Of the seas.
"There's the shore!"
Exclaims the Soul
As she stands up
And walks through the
crushing waves
Onto the wet sand.
It was only a few feet away,
Waiting for her

Heart's obeisance.
"Thank you, my Lord
God," the Soul says humbly.
"You are welcome,"
He says as Him-Self,
Manifested
And manifesting
The pinkest dawn
Spreading rising Light
Over sea and shore,
Radiating all His creatures
From within.

Eternity

Happy is the one
Who, leaning on the Invisible
One, loses the Self
In the All.
Happy is the one who,

Leaving the shores
Of the familiar known,
Crosses over to the Oneness
Of Eternity.
Happy are we who,
Clinging to our sacred
Humanity, fed by the eternal
Springs of salvation,
Find the shores of Oneness
Within our own hearts.

For the one who loses
The self
In the verdant meadows of certainty
Can never go back
To the unknowing vales
Of confusion.

Lose thyself, therefore,
Humbly, in the all-encompassing
Embrace of His Love,

And let no one hinder thee
From that Remembrance
Of the Eternal Lover.

One Day of God

When each of the Prophets
Brought the Holy Word,
Time stood still, hearts obeyed,
The Prophecy to fulfill.

Leaving behind mere egos,
All peoples fell down to pray,
Then stood up, steadfast in heart,
To follow Thy Holy Ways:

One infinite Day, divinely freeing,
Gift from Wisdom's tongue,
Day of God blessing each Being
--Mystery where we're One.

Whatever their life-lessons—
Parent, teacher, trades—
They emptied their hands of trinkets;
His Love all loves replace.

When the Breath from on
High blew down,
Divinity's Message lifted,
Unity's Presence was announced
To live the life that's gifted.

One long Day, infinite Way,
Gift from the Merciful One.
Day of God blesses each Being—
Mystery where we're One.

What Wonder

What wonder art Thou to pour forth
From Thy inimitable Heart
Love and Mercy for Thy creatures
Beyond anything they deserve.

What immensity of Kindness
Cascades from Thy eternal Essence,
Creating worlds-upon-worlds
Past all reckoning.

What gratefulness we must feel,
Realizing that every
particle of beingness
Is a direct result of Thy Mystery—
The Source of all life everywhere.

Please accept, therefore, our gratitude
For the Unity Thou hast created
Through all Thy Manifestations,
Which is how we understand

That we are One.

Renewal

Without the Love of the Creator
Everything turns to dust:

The blooming flower of the Soul
Withers like a rose
In the scorching sun.

The green sapling standing
Straight and tall
Droops, old and yellow-leaved.

The hungry bluebird chick
Peeps haplessly in its nest,
Waiting for a parent to return.

All feed from the same
Wondrous Source—
The fountaining Love of God.

Let go, then, of that which
no longer serves,
Material desires or spiritual
attachments,
While the clear waves of Love

Wash heart and mind,
Bowing the Soul in nearness
To the King of Kings.

Questions

When the wind blows
Across the water,
Bringing waves of bliss
From the horizon edge
Of eternity,
A new dawn comes
That lights the Earth
With a new, holy Light.

Myriads of celestial voices
Sing the praise of the One
Who brings order
To chaos,
And Love to disharmony.
Without that wonderment,
Life becomes meaningless.

Breathe in the breeze
Of contentment!
Feel the ocean waters
Of Life tickling your toes!
There is no time but the present
To begin the process
Of Soul-diving—plunging
Deep into your Self
And asking,
"Who am I
As you have made me,
Dear Creator,
And why am I here—
At this time—on this planet,
With my eternal companion?
What are we meant to do,
In the broader scheme of things,
As we advance, step-by-sturdy-

Step, towards the Oneness
Of all Life
And the eternity
Of Thy Love?"

Take the Impossible Journey

Beyond the farthest shore,
Past the farthest horizon,
In the midmost Heart
Of the Universe,
Resides the Point of Return.
Free thy-Self of all impediments
And advance towards the Tree
Beyond which there is no passing
Where the New World opens up—
Spread out in the Glory of Infinity!

Do not question Its existence:
Eternal Life awaits each one
Who lets the Self be lifted
In the Embracing Arms of Love.
Wait for no one and advance
Towards the Unknowable Essence
That can never be reached—
Yet always resides within.

Without a Doubt

Listen closely, my dear one.

Today
The Merciful Eye
Views our hearts,
Scans our Soul
So compassionately
We out-run
Our dusty past.

Arching over the river
Like willows, we bend
Beneath a breeze of Joy,
Opening
Our blushing Selves
Like roses
In the gentle downpour
Of Love.

Do not regret the past—
Simply welcome the present
Moment of Joy
When we may embrace
The enormity of This Love
Of All the Ages.

Overcoming the Faces of Prejudice

It pains and burdens the heart to acknowledge, as well as to stand by and remain passive for so long, in light of the continuing problem afflicting all of the political, socio-economic, and religious models as presently organized, practiced, and experienced, reflecting their incompatible structures and patterns throughout time, antagonistic and contrary to the fundamentals of justice and unity, as established, time-and-again, by the Manifestations of God.

These subtleties of the heart can no longer be afforded the ignoring and ineffectual approach at solving their insidious nature and damage. Just like sexual abuse and harassment was brought to light in an explosive way in both the secular and religious environments, heavily weighted by litigations and the financial costs of individual or group remunerations, we do not want to wait any longer and experience a sudden burst of a collective anger towards those who have, for a long time, practiced behind the veils of "glass ceilings" behavior and actions that distort, delay, and impede the spiritual and material growth of all of our members.

We cannot fall in the well of commonality both in behavior and patterns and yet claim to bring the elixir of change to humanity's travails. It is both insensitive and a travesty, deceptive and the continuation of lies to pretend that everything is just fine.

Once the veils are lifted that prevent the true understanding of our human Purpose and its overwhelming significance, in the light of a progressive and timely release to come of Divine Knowledge, and its effects on the population, the people will inevitably, rise up, using extremely painful and violent methods, against all practices not totally aligned with justice and equity among all the ethnic groups, large or small, cultures, religions, and genders extant upon the Earth.

Recently we have experienced how the sexual abuse within religion's institutions, entertainment, work-place, and other organizations has been exposed. The time comes when the Light illumines the darkest corners of the human heart.

It is understood that the malady in question,

prejudice, pre-exists the formative age of all Dispensations of Divine Information. Nonetheless, we must be vigilant and begin to acknowledge and address its practices within our institutions. We should no longer tolerate its presence and do absolutely nothing to prevent its practice, especially when it relates to a certain cultural root. In a world of names and appearances, we should be careful that we do not reflect one religion, rather than the world-Faith of God—an integrated and unified instrumentality for good, as well as for the advancement of civilization.

We must remove the cob-webs from our eyes, and face God's Manifestations directly, naked and exposed to the Healing, Purifying Light of our Oneness, as mature entities, letting go all fears based on false conceptions of illusory differences, and the conditioning, over time, creating disharmony among us.

By an over-emphasis on the historical beginnings of any One of the Creator's Expressions, thereby de-emphasizing the actual Words of God as the Transformative Principle, religious organizations become spiritless, without the elixir of change. Further, by elevating within such organizations those persons who trace their ancestry to a particular culture, or are of a particular racial or educational background, those leading such organizations weaken their structure, and go against the original intent of the Founder of such a community of the called.

This imbalance has led to a hidden agenda within these religious organizations, where those in power assert an inherently destructive use of privilege and rank. The insidious consequence is separation and injustice, a tearing-apart of the very fabric of Unity established and envisioned by God's Manifestations, and substituted instead the varying levels of political maneuvering now controlling the world's belief systems.

As such, these institutions will, over time, become the greatest obstacle and enemy of <u>He Who brings the next Revelation of God's Will and Pleasure</u>. We are cookie-cutting believers in the name of expediency, foregoing the individual's divine right for <u>independent investigation</u> of God's Faith, ignoring thus one of the most basic principles of truth-based reliance, as delineated in science.

Without the supreme emphasis on the <u>mystical</u>

bestowal upon each Soul-possessing Being of Light through the original Divine Word, regardless of that entity's outward appearance from genetic or environmental modulations, how do we justly implement the Faith of God as mature entities? Without honoring each being's unique Knowingness, as a servant to the All-Knowing One, and as a contributor to a divine civilization, how can humanity as a whole grow in its spiritual station?

Let's face it. We should be careful in how any Revelation's Program of Change is delivered, as It conditions (encodes) human understanding and subsequent behavior. Those who promulgate the revised and continuing Divine Story, an enhanced Spiritual Script, with its evolving roles and services, rituals and emerging traditions, while simultaneously dismissing earlier practices and roles, should bear in mind the populace's divine right for dependence on none other than the Creator (Manifested), as we "read" our own books of life.

Trusting thus the Divine Plan and God's Messengers, Who continue to oversee Its development, in part through religious institutions, in the light of what is just, we must understand that the guided governance of even the most devoted humans depends on their hearts' purity and their clear-mindedness. Those who govern a Faith's administrative affairs, must also understand that their roles and positions do not mean they are given free rein to "control," and thus hierarchically to manipulate any potentially transformative outcome. Shunning any personal, vested interests in the way they design their programs, they should avoid activities whose sole purpose is to increase the membership for the financial support of the institution. Further, they ought not deny those mystic knowers would teach the Message of the Founder, for by doing so these administrative heads would be invalidating the personal, mystical experiences of Souls lit from within.

How the Whole process becomes integrated, and clearly designed and defined as a vibrant, strong, and functional system, will in the end prove our present inadequacy and obstinacy, lack of obedience to God's Law, and resistance to being transformed. We blindly follow the few who insist there is only one way to lead the march towards a spiritually-purposeful, clear-minded, and pure-hearted humanity doing the right things, and living the right way. Yet, haven't we failed before, time-and-again, using just this type of programming, in which the need for the enlightenment of the individual is conditioned and subsumed under the need of the institution to keep existing.

***

As we are reminded of our chance to do things differently, and move towards our collective maturity, respectful of an independent and inter-dependent approach as seekers of the Truth—knowing that God does what He Wills and Pleases, on whomever He chooses—let us understand the need for those independent thinkers that feed the seeds of caution and adjustment to a community of servants.

Over time there surfaces, so far back in our history that it is best to say it has always been a part of our human predisposition, a tendency and inclination to feel better than others, giving birth to the many faces of a spiritual myopia. This condition can also be described as bigotry, bias, intolerance, narrow-mindedness, or just plain prejudice.

It is a spiritual phenomenon, resulting from an incomplete understanding of being human—of knowing,

Who am I? Why am I here? Where did I come from? Where am I going?

Disconnected from its Root and Source, humanity is far from its non-physical beginning, and therefore is influenced by ideas, unconstrained by time and space, contagious as a disease, that move from heart-to-heart instilling separation, disunity, and violence, until the entire species is imprisoned within delusions that justify its self-destructive practices.

As groups are born, bringing about families, villages, towns, cities, nations, and civilizations, generations fall prey to these egoic and environmental modulations. People allow their base feelings to influence their characters and basic nature. Perceiving the world in terms of "us versus them" appears to be a reasonable and realistic way to deal with surface appearances and differences among the creatures of One Creator.

Without embracing a deep understanding of how unity is the basis of all diverse life, we pass on, from one-to-the-next generation, erroneous viewpoints, so that whole groups of people end up being swallowed within a black hole of disenfranchisement. No one questions the validity and reasonableness of these thought-forms. Instead, myriads succumb to this destructive programming, resulting in a totally distorted way of living affecting the whole of the system of life and intelligence on the planet.

We, as spiritual entities, are incarcerated within these distorted designs—the scripts and roles of our lives—in cultures that emphasize their expressions. Our resultant conditioning and patterns expand to form chaotic and ugly societal forms and structures. These emerging socio-economic and political models of leadership and governance flow through every aspect of life: affecting families, communities, cities, nations, and the world we all live in.

The dysfunction does not stop there. Instead, it is exported everywhere, and since human interaction has become a global experience beyond its linear (time-wise) and local expressions, it has emerged and flooded all of our virtual worlds and modes of communication—minds and hearts.

Thus, without borders or distances to travel, spaces to contain its depravity and insidious nature, this spiritual myopia has entered the minds and hearts of all its inhabitants, the players and actors, and their games played. The cacophony from inharmonious thoughts, feelings, and actions afflicts the scientists, the spiritual leaders, those in power, in fact, every Soul-possessing creature. Inundated by this "spiritual noise," all those known as "human" by agreement, all members of the planetary Spirit of Life and Intelligence who call the Earth their home, become agents of injury to the surrounding life, unable to realize or express their True Potential as Beings of Light.

Furthermore, since the Spirit of Life and Intelligence exerts its influence through imperceptible fields of activity (the Spirit of the Universe), it extends invisibly throughout this Simulation of Life, a Workshop for entities to grow spiritually. So, locally, those Soul-possessing Beings on Earth who are <u>not attuned</u> to the proper resonance of Beauty given by the Source of All (known as the Divine Spirit) affect all others through this unified field of all possibilities, infecting all of creation (though often unwittingly) with the jangling assault of chaotic frequencies. We are all One!

So many groups or associations, created over time, have become diseased at the root, from their formations on. Nothing has been left untouched wherever and whenever humans come together. In one form or another, the ugly faces of prejudice emerge throughout all interactions and exchanges. Some of these appearances are easily discoverable. Others are far more insidious, hidden deep within the layering that makes the actuality we all experience. In the end, we are all suffering both the consequences of prejudice, and its repercussions over time, as the doors of spiritual growth and opportunity do not welcome everyone. These manifest and hidden distortions bring about separation and disunity outwardly, and an inner discomfort and distress, disquiet and fear—disturbing the minds and hearts of everyone!

How can we talk about this "us versus them" mentality, an attitude and intention based upon appearances and descriptions underlying all prejudicial viewpoints and opinions, when its sheer mention to anyone often causes an eruption—a response charged with anger and accusatory remarks, threats of expulsion from one's group, followed by public condemnation? Furthermore, the victims of prejudice are framed as its perpetrators, and the breakers of the status quo are falsely accused of being the disruptors of the underlying Unity, when, in fact, this Unity given by our Creator's Manifestations is a totally different Script.

It is this Divine Script that is meant to be practiced, leading to life-supporting roles that must be maintained. Were we to utilize clarifying, open discussions, grounded in pure and loving objectives, in an atmosphere of mutual respect, fairness, and justice, we would create lasting solutions to problems themselves only generated from each individual's disconnection from the Soul and Spirit of all Life and Intelligence.

Slaves to the pernicious influences of our environments—indoctrinated, manipulated, controlled, and subdued like a herd of sheep—we lurch forward without a compass towards an unknown destination.

Upholding hierarchies within our "spiritual" institutions; placing people in power because of accepted ancestry, cultural background, education, gender, race, or material wealth; we dishonor those qualities making us human: clarity of mind, purity of heart, a righteous and compassionate character, and an attitude of service to all life everywhere—without exception.

The sacred theater of life has become a cheap horror-show, permeated by such inequality and injustice within our species that Baha'u'llah, Prophet

Founder of the Baha'i Faith, foresaw and lamented its occurrence more than a century and a half ago.

The poisonous plant of prejudice—buttressed by the "glass ceilings" existing within every large organization or societal structure, which allow only the privileged few to be given full access to material power, wealth, and inside information—bends the minds and hearts of the people towards division and hatred.

This ancient evil of prejudice must be recognized. Then the solution is clear.

Plant the Tree of Acceptance within by connecting to the One Root—the Soul and Spirit linking us all as the divine reflections of the Great Being.

It is simply a matter of reconditioning and

perception—a new global Script. All the Holy, Chosen Ones have reminded us—we are creatures of One Creator, with One Divine Purpose: to Remember and Return to our True Station as Soul-possessing, Spirit Beings of Light.

Remembering thus, together we may cast into the dust the shackles of delusionary divisions, and arise as One to manifest the Beauty in the Garden of the Heart of God.

Flying Before the Storm

Like the wedge of geese
That flies through the cloudy sky,
We take our turns leading
With kindness and compassion.
The work never ceases.

Sometimes we tire, threaten
To drop down from mist-
filled, lofty realms,
When the sky-echoing calls
Recall us to the task—

Keep moving the wings,
Stretching out pointed
beak and long neck
Behind our feathered family until
Again, it's our turn

To face the full onslaught
Of the storm wind's resistance,
Strive until, all together, we land
Atop the blessedly clean water.

Morning Vision

This morning I rode the
back of a heron

Between two wings of white.
Sailing through blue,
upon a cool breeze,
Lost in Mystery of the Flight.

Held in the Arms of Love,
Feeling Freedom's taste,
If only our cloudy hearts would rain,
Clearing all time and space.

No one is "better" than anyone else.
We're oaks rooted in One Soul.
Follow the flight of angels
To find where the world should go.

Circling Within
the Breath

Listen deep within
To the heart-beat of Life.

It beats out a rhythm
That destroys dis-unity,
Encourages Oneness—
Little-by-little.
It is the sound of a seed
Cracking open to let
The tiny, two-leaf seedling
Poke its delicate head
Above the rich, brown soil.
It is the whispering, mysterious
Song of a hidden Bird
Waking the Dawn
With the Remembrance
of celestial Melodies.
<u>Listen My Love</u>,
Calls softly
To the ear of the heart.
<u>There can be no loneliness</u>
<u>When I am nearby</u>.
Like a mother softly caressing
Her new-born

Against her breast,
Come closer to me, softly says
The All-Knowing One.
The Song of Life
Is My Song,
Floating in-and-out
Of My Mysterious Being
On My Ever-present Breath.

Workers of the Light

At every point of entry throughout the Sea of Awareness, we find enlightened entities counseling and guiding, performing the work that brings solutions, clarity of mind, and tranquility of heart. To the casual observer, these activities may not make sense, for they do not share similar degrees or conditions defining their Knowingness and Lovingness. The dissimilarities of communication, and understanding, and the many variations in the states of the Heart are such, that for all appearances, a planetary system of Life and Intelligence seems to harbor myriads of alien, mind-world constructs that may be likened to the sand grains of all the beaches in the world.

Despite these many chromatic variations of the Light illumining all the hearts of its inhabitants, the workers of the Light pursue one goal, to be channels that bring, however dim or bright in its intensity, the necessary Illumination, from its Source, allowing those that live and interact an opportunity to advance to higher levels of conscious-awareness.

Whatever needs to be done, through whatever Heart Language may be required, and through whatever means possible, the Light-worker is there in response to those that plead for assistance, through the Mercy of God, which is always there to succor those that reach out of the darkness of their hearts.

The Sea of Awareness contains all of Creation. All Life and Intelligence that has found expression and exists is immersed and bathed from within it. It is what gives meaning to the understanding that our Creator is the Lord of all the worlds of True Understanding and Divine Love. This omni-dimensional and multi-directional state of awareness is ever-present everywhere. It is the Source and the Effect of all Divine thoughts and feelings, communications that uplift and succor, and actions that advance civilization. This awareness defines us, our True Selves and nature. It is sensed as a Oneness of Being with the All. It seeks to express its Divine Message in worlds of time through our thoughts and feelings, words and actions, that manifest naturally from the ever-present sense of Justice and Unity.

It is a Mirror reflecting the Will and Pleasure of the Creator. It is the Soul of all the entities ever created.

As Soul-possessing creatures, all traveling entities manifest the many variations of their Spiritual development as inner understandings and states of Love, throughout each and all sojourns in worlds of time. The Light-workers emerge, here-and-there, as effects of a stage in their development of the Knowingness and Lovingness necessary to assist those within the range of their influence. Through moments of interaction and connection, fifth-, fourth-, and third- dimensionally speaking, using Spirit, mind, and body, they are guided to assess and share the Love and Knowledge from the Ancient of Days.

Most people are unaware of the degree and quality of their connectivity to the Root-Source of their state and wholeness—giving significance to the Purpose of Creation in the words: <u>My creatures are My Mystery. I Am their Mystery</u>.

We have all returned to worlds of time, and beyond that, have disclosed the necessary attributes that allow for an amicable Reunion with the Beloved of all the worlds. These sojourns eventually awaken and resurrect entities to the recognition and acceptance of He Who God makes Manifest, during those beings' emergence on the shores of consciousness.

Beginning with the contrast between what is right and what is wrong, and the Law governing existence everywhere, travelers are guided towards righteousness and caring. Thereby, these humble beings become the conscious recipients of His Divine Love, while knowing of the eternal worlds of Revelation that await each servant seeking the Great Being's Mercy.

There are myriad degrees of Understanding within one drop of water from the Sea of Awareness, sufficing the eternal Spiritual growth of the seeker of Truth. Merging with that Sea of Awareness becomes the goal of every creature in Creation.

Moving On

Below the sky
And above the land,
In the in-between place
Of Mystery,
Past the fog of ignorance,
Lies the clear air
Of Knowledge
Where we must soar.

Like the hawk aloft
On wings of grace,
We wait patiently
For the dawn sun
To arise—
Lighting up all that is good:

The flowers un-budding,
The trees shaking green leaves
In a cool, summer breeze,
And the babies laughing
When devoted parents
Shower them with love.

There is no time
Like the heart-full
Present where we wait
As patiently as we can
For Spring
Spreading new, green shoots

Across the dusty,
disintegrating leaves
Of the fallen season:

Time
To fold our wings, let go,
With one, shivering movement,
The dust
Of lifetimes.

Bee Teachers

Busy lady workers
Pollinate every flower.
No matter what color is the weed—
Pollen is the power!

Keeping all the creatures
Surrounded by growing things,
Busy bees are happy,
Full of viv and spring.

Let's all plant our yards full
Of plants bees are enjoying—
Clover and wild sassafras,
No pesticides, no poison.

Humans want to live.
Insects do as well.
Four-leggeds, wing-ed ones,
And plants all need their spell.

Striped magicians as they fly
Well-dressed in glittering pollen
Are like a thousand Atlases
Lifting those who've fallen.

Close-by

Across the deep blue ocean,
Beyond the mountainous sky,
Lives a land of enduring Love
Where not a Soul can die.

To this land we all return
When leaving mortality's nest,
Welcomed by God's clear radiance,
That words cannot express.

In this new life the Heart reigns,
Nor is there a drop of fear.
Blessed Beings rejoice everywhere—
God's Will forever steers.

Yet why wait to dwell there?
This place is wonderfully near.
Surrender the self to the Merciful One,
And embrace sweet life so dear.

The Longest Journey

Who knows how long we have been
On this Journey to the Sun of Truth?
Who can tell
When the sky was born,

The seas poured down,
And the Earth risen up
For plants and animals to flourish?
Why people were allowed
To inhabit a Garden
So perfect
That one wrong word
Could wilt a legion
Of purple pansies?
This gift of ever-lasting life,
So many stops
On the endless trail of possibilities
Cannot ever have an end—
Or a beginning.
The Omniscient One knows
That every stop
And start
Is necessary for the Soul's growth,
The way a rose bush
Of pink, fragrant blossoms
Shows-off its beauty in the Spring

And the Summer, and begins
To hide it-self
In the Fall and Winter.

Why not let this time of growth
Spread everywhere
Like seeds in the wind?
Here-and-there,
On rocky soil and on rich compost,
They will bury themselves.
Unexpectedly, months later,
The first, green shoots
Will toss about their grassy heads,
Grateful for the chance to
Live life again,
Closer to the Sun.

Freeing the Heart

Blossoming, Blossoming
Is the Heart

When the Lord doth call.
Don't wait a second to turn
To Him—let all else
Fall.
The trumpet sound is loud and clear.
Other sounds fade to
Silence.
The Lord's sweet voice
Resounds like thunder
Throughout the Lands
Abiding.
"Time waits for no one,"
So they say, but what do they know
Of Truth hiding?
When it's God Who comes calling,
Time stops,
Love shines,
Unfailing.

Sea Depths

Beneath the sand
Of the watery canyon
Where the last bit of light spins
Like a toy
Through creation's portal,

Transforming
To
Realms of Joy,

The All-Knowing One awaits us
With His Love.

There is nothing like this Radiance.

Though we attempt,
We cannot ask for His Embrace
Without surrendering all else:

Other loves, enmities,
devotional practices even
Love consumes
Until nothing is left except

Wings fluttering
In the dazzling Light—

The Soul's bright butterflies
Rising like tiny angels above
banks of blood-red roses
One early, spring morning.

Out of the Sea of Awareness emerge numberless
carrier waves, each an individual moment on its
own track of time, seamlessly coalescing into the
fabric of an actuality that carries slowed down
packets of frequencies that together bring the
beauty of creation. As we see and experience this
wondrous, bidirectional flow, spiraling to-and-fro

in a non-linear time of multi-directions and omni-dimensional tonalities of depth in space, a richness of form and sound, of movement and apparent stillness, we are captivated by, and in awe of, the infinity of pleasure riding upon these waves of creation. Everywhere our awareness swims, the feeling of Divine Love embraces us.

The Sea of Awareness was there before us, and will be there after each of us leaves a world of time. As travelers, we emerge onto the shores of consciousness from that Sea of Awareness. Holding all potentials in transit and transcendence, we are conduits for creation itself to flow from its dormant, unmanifested oneness of being something, anything, towards its manifested unity, of everything always.

This super-positioning of diverse tracks of

time upon seamlessly integrated and orchestrated carrier waves makes for continuous communication among all existence, back-and-forth, throughout distances measured in light years, nanoseconds, and everything in-between.

There is harmony and complementarity out of a chaos that is brought to order, within a relativity created by diverse systems of life and intelligence in their own time-and-space constructs throughout, down to the intricacies of cause-and-effect.

Such is the fabric of a reality built within a Simulator and Trainer that serves all traveling entities, human by agreement, Soul-possessing, Spirits of Life and Intelligence during their sojourns in worlds of time. As each traveler grows in spiritual understanding, he or she comes to know the intricacies within this

Divine System, that integrates, manages, schedules, regulates, and sustains itself throughout creation.

The quality and seamlessness, or not, of the traveler's integration with this Whole express his or her degree of Spiritual development. The higher and more complete such an integration is with the pre-existing natural state of a planetary system of life and intelligence, the more useful is one's contribution to the overall advancement of a cooperating collective. The less integrated (within and without) that individuals are, the more those beings contribute to the degradation and destruction of their environments, as well as to the disharmony of the finely-tuned, infinitely-connected Whole of creation.

One way or another, every visiting entity, in

the end, will learn and develop the thought-forms, feelings, communicating skills, behavior, and actions suitable for his or her graduation away from the cycles of life and death—and from the returns to worlds of time.

Letting Go

Everything desires Thy Love,
O my God.
From kitchen sprouts in a glass jar,
To spiraling, golden galaxies.

Though taller than
Tibetan mountains,
What treasure outweighs
Thy Blessings?

With Thy compassion and grace
Born beyond realms On High,

Overflow my heart
So I may walk fearlessly,

Carrying out Thy Will,
For Thee,
The dust of old desires
Spinning across the road:

Brown, crumpled Leaves
Moving like the skeletons
Of tiny, drunken animals
In autumn breezes.

Unfolding

Inside the Heart of Love
Is another Heart
And another, infinitely smaller
And more intense—concentrated
Love that disappears
Into a Dot

Of Knowingness.
This Dot is you,
Encompassing everything!

Let the One, Mysterious
Word of God
Explode open
That Point of Return
So that everything
Becomes nothing
In His Eyes.

(Ya Baha'ul'abha)
The Glory of the Point
Is found
In Infinity.

Ask yourself these questions: Who am I? Where am I? Why am I here? Where did I come from? Where am I going?

The Truth of it All depends upon the answers.

A Prayer to the Lord

O Lord,
Let my heart be kind,
My soul be pure,
My mind be clear
Of anything save Thy Will.

O Lord,
Let my hands do good deeds,
My feet walk upon Thy Path,
My heart beat to the rhythm
Of Thy Breath.
O Lord,
Let my mind be filled
With the radiant, blue sky
Of Thy Heavenly Knowingness,
And may I share

With the world
Thy Love and Understanding
So that All Peoples
May look up to Thee
And raise their voices in Thy Praise.

These questions open up the heart, the seat of the Soul and connection to God, Source of All. This connectivity to the Root-level brings into play the Creative Force engaging Life and Intelligence, balancing the tug-of-war between the mind and heart. What we desire and how we think are transformed by this well-grounded approach and process allowing the positive flow of creativity to accomplish its intended objective without the short-comings and incomplete experiences too common in people's life.

Again, strive for the purity of heart and clarity of

mind to receive from On High the answers to these questions:

Who am I?

Why am I here?

Where am I?

Where do I come from?

Where am I going?

Having their answers fulfills both our hearts and our minds, bringing the needed tranquility during the unfoldment of our purpose in the here-and-now. The answers contain many levels of meaning. In answering the question, 'where am I?', for instance, though at first it seems clear that we're living upon the planet Earth, yet, aren't we actually existing within a much greater Whole?

Living in a world of time, we're part of a huge system of Life and Intelligence containing universes, within a Simulator and Trainer giving all of us the opportunities to develop our Spiritual Natures so that we can <u>leave</u> that reflection of Reality, eventually, and enter into eternal worlds of Revelation.

When we develop our hearts and minds simultaneously, in a balanced way, we grow spiritually. Our understanding of the Whole, in keeping with our roles as individuals, builds relationships well-oriented towards all living creatures, including ourselves. Able to perceive the truth in any situation, and act in an orderly fashion, we take responsibility for our feelings, thoughts, communication, and actions, as well as take into consideration the feelings and thoughts of others.

When we ignore our hearts, by-passing our ability to feel and care, we cut off the flow of Life that runs throughout the planet. Soon enough, we become more-and-more disconnected from it all. To be selfishly aloof is simply not really to care about anything, including about one's Self.

When this effect, brought about by our disconnection, becomes what most individuals experience and act from on a daily basis, the world and all life become a nightmare. Within the Dream or Desire of the Creator, the Simulation of Life and Intelligence made up of endless worlds of time in which we live, physically, we can no longer serve our Purpose. Without meaning in our lives, lost within our egoic-selves, longing for any way out, we grasp at any solutions.

Addictions bring the many attachments and distractions that wear and tear the body and the mind, in a whirlpool of disordered emotions that further eat away at the core of our nature and the true-reason for being here.

Removed farther-and-farther away from the intended, eternal companionship of lovers sharing an amicable, ever-present Reunion with the Beloved that lives within each of us, we find ourselves in a hellish environ far from any dream within the Creator's Dream, spiraling downwards towards non-existence where everything is disassembling and dying.

All of our actions and effects that appear to be constructive at first, in the end are brought to nothing in a sea of a chaotic turmoil that all of our negative emotions have brought to bear, channeled from within, and rained down on a theater no longer of life.

The heart and mind must be balanced to act as the fulcrum of the pairing phenomenon of males and females. The weft of wisdom must be woven on the warp of love, as a viable means-to-the-end of Returning to our Source. We must reverse course, so that the ship of Life and Intelligence of creation sails before the fruitful breath of our true destiny— sustaining and advancing a Divine and Eternal civilization.

Though having lost its way long ago, our kind must now embrace the Life and Intelligence meant to adorn its human frame.

Not So Far

Behind the pink clouds
Lives another world.
Here every being savors Light,
Imbibes Joy.
Here the young never get old,
Those old in wisdom
Rejoice in the praises
Of God—the All-Knowing—
And every heart is filled
With the over-flowing
Fountain of Love.

Each heart knows
When it must know
The way to live,
Eternally.
"How may I arrive
At this land of Light?"
You ask.

It is within, deep within,
And simply waits for the door
To the ego to be shut,
And the door to God's Love
To be opened.

Communications

To speak with one another and to feel the Love flowing back-and-forth, connecting at deeper levels, is a sign of caring, respect, responsibility, and joint effort in sustaining the growth of any relationship. By being there, always and throughout the conversation, recalling the privilege of the friendship, savoring the moment of union, and reflecting later on what was said with a smile, we demonstrate our unity with God's Purpose for His creatures.

In looking forward to seeing each other again, exchanging precious thoughts while immersed in each other's lives, being able to recall a detail from a past conversation, sharing a smile and the sincere laughter of friends in telling a story begun long ago, being supportive of each other during difficulties for as long as it takes, we exhibit our True Nature as Soul-possessing, Spirit Beings of Light.

Such is the way of sharing in a divine setting permeated with the Love of God. Recognizing and appreciating the value of existence and each other, we appreciate each moment together as a gift given by Spirit. Nothing else is important enough to interrupt this opportunity to continue growing together. Lovers of Truth, we savor the affection and caressing, even the touch of words, as our hearts fill with a joy that continually invites and endears us to each other. The desire to meet, again-and-again, charms the flow of time, as silent smiles and gentle eyes hold us in a redolent space of eternity.

Feeding the Fire

Inside each Being
Is a spark of Joy
That must be fed
From the Inimitable One!
Feed it with Divine Love,
With Compassion,
With Hope,
With the Knowingness
That God is always
Here
For all of us.

The spark
Will roar into Life—
Lighting-up the Soul
With the fire that burns not,
Illuminating each,
Precious creature
With the Creator's Gift

Of Oneness:
Uniting all life everywhere,
For-ever,
The Blessing
Of the Sun's Light
Penetrating everything
With Radiance.

Spring Showers

When the last breath's taken,
The Soul released in a sigh,
Rejoicing peals from heaven:
True Union is close-by.

But why wait for that final moment?
The Lord leans closer than flowers.
Sink into nothingness within,
Find Eternity blossoming power.

There is nothing you can't attain,
If pure with a humble heart.
Bow in the Presence of Bliss-rains,
Lifted-up in His Breeze, unmarred.

The Light

Beyond the Rainbow's Colors
In the farthest point of sky
Lives a point of wondrous Light
Akin to Creator's Eye.

This Portal to Knowingness,
Immortality above,
Lives within each of us,
While filling Realms with Love.

Cleaning with compassion,
This Light replaces shadow.
Though all lives appear to end,
It strengthens every marrow.

For why would God give a Gift
That fades like any flower?
Our Soul roots in Eternity—
Our dwelling of Beauty and Power!

Beloved Companions

When two hearts unite as One,
God's Sea of Love overflows.
Upon each Being Soul-unified
Unnumbered blessings He bestows.

From swirling galaxies of stars
He's plucked these two companions,
Two beaming points merged to a Star
To light-up distant canyons.

All praise to the All-Knowing One
Who brings Eternity nigh:
These waves immortal Oceans make,
Lit by the Dawn-bright Sky.

Safe Return

Letting go is easy
When fruit is past its prime.
Just place it in the weedy grass
To compost for a time.

Holding on is harder
When the gift cannot be seen.
Can we cling to eddying wind
From Wings that spark and gleam?

God sends each precious Being
Sailing to different shores,
Though the same Breeze
brings us back—
The Soul is Home to all.

Before all else, the entity begins to communicate with his or her higher Self. Through these intimate communiques, the birthing egoic-self begins to acquire form and place, to stand his or her ground in the midst of protesting reminders from within, as conscience comes to life, bridging the higher, Divine Realm to a lower world of time.

As one's "I-ness" takes hold of its mortal existence—the fractional and temporal flow of experiences that grounds the traveler to a fixed address within a physiological structure—he or she learns to be comfortable within its skin.

The range of an entity's expressions, in response to an environ outside his or her egoic-self, begins the conditioning and programming that emerges as an identity, with scripts and roles that help determine the type of participation within a society, a tribe to fit in, and serve with, in ever-progressing ways.

Communication becomes the way to fulfill the deep desire to know and be known, to love and be loved.

This individual process of spiritual growth catapults the traveler into greater-and-greater realms of influence over a life-time—from the family, to the community, to the city-state, to the nation, and finally to the world. Concomitantly, the sojourner's observations and participations become the understanding of each moment, expressed eventually through eternal relationships that speed God's servants along the Pathway to the Source of all.

One of the most divisive practices humanity has developed and employed is through the creation and practice of special groups or "insiders" within organizations. Those individuals "in the know," or "for your eyes only," use restrictive communiques with the words "classified or secret." This nomenclature emphasizes discrimination, suspicion, isolation, investigation, distrust, etc., justifiable within a planetary System of Life and Intelligence whose inhabitants live and experience the effects of lives in violation of the code of righteousness. When traveling entities play myriad, ego-based games, they become conditioned, or programmed to interact in ways contrary to the dictates of their Higher Selves.

When this practice occurs within larger, planetary communities and beyond, acting against the Divine Plan's purpose of promoting Unity and Oneness, it creates negative ramifications and influence upon the collective, spiritual growth. At a minimum, any possible benefits, in terms of tranquility and sustainability, to the relationships within and among cultures globally, is delayed.

Over time, every race of inhabitants is meant to learn to share, cooperate, and live together amicably.

So called "glass ceilings," in which some individuals obtain privileges over others, have appeared everywhere. We see this discrimination practiced between the male and female genres, within families, communities, cities, states, and nations. This practice has also shown its prejudicial face in religions and business, politics, the military, all governments of all nations, and non-governmental organizations including lodges, fraternities, academia, all sports, and the entertainment industry. In fact, everywhere individuals gather and interact has been subject to dysfunction through disunity.

This divisionary practice does not come about randomly. When it begins, it is seeded into an organization through a vital and critical, orderly plan expressing this subtle, evil intention. The plan must be in place early in a group's formation, after which it gathers importance over time. Like all social diseases, it is endemic and addictive, ending always in some form of separation, destruction, and even violence towards the people within, or outside a particular group. In extreme cases, those who expose the evil existence of prejudice are killed.

Those "in the know," at the top of organizations infected with the evil of prejudice, are secretive and extremely careful. They monitor all communications, directing the most important information only to others in the know.

This evil infects personal relationships at a more intimate level as well, including marriages, friendships, and work relations. Here discrimination often takes the form of avoidance. Additionally, individuals may use special, non-verbal signals or specialized language, recognizable only to those in the inner circle. They may even use a foreign language from another culture that those considered of lesser status in their organization cannot understand. This evil practice has risen to become commonplace, and is often found in religious centers, or other gatherings, seemingly structured for the purpose of disseminating altruistic services.

The attitude of "us versus them" grows as the population increases, and is thus prevalent in all societies. This practice keeps disunity alive and well, swelling its size and kind, eventually leading to conflict and war.

Lies and Truth

How do you distinguish a lie
From the Truth?
A lie shuts the heart
Like a huge, wooden castle door
Locked with iron fasteners.
The Truth opens the heart
Like a spring meadow
Of wild flowers—all colors
Of butterflies meandering
Among them.
A lie cuts friendship
Like a razor—tattered
Feelings thrown like rags
Upon the dusty ground.
The Truth binds companions

Eternally—clothing them
In the royal, ruby-red robes
Of Love.
Lies grow from the soil
Of fear and grief.
Truth grows from ever-present
Love, blossoming Joy.
Choose Truth, dear ones,
And on its soaring Wings
Return Home.

It is our spiritual duty to see all entities as merely reflections of our Higher Selves, led by the Soul-based point of view. As we develop the virtues, or Divine Attributes, within us—such as compassion, kindness, and unconditional Love—we view all <u>others</u> as not separate from our-Selves. Integrated within, we understand the Truth that all creatures are equally dependent upon One Creator for their very existence.

All are fed by the same infinite Well of Love from the Unknowable Essence, through the Manifestations of the Source of all Life everywhere—within worlds of creation and worlds of Revelation.

We are each walking upon a unique, individual path, yet, as the Native Americans say, we are all indivisibly linked in one, delicate yet incredibly strong, web of life. Despite the intricacies of the systems of omni-dimensional realities within, and outside of, temporal worlds, the basis of spiritual life is simple—treat others as you wish to be treated, and love God beyond all else. If all entities were to fulfill those two dictums, all realities would reflect the infinite Beauty of God's Kingdom.

God laughs when creatures
Think they're gods, forgetting Who
Makes their destiny.

Books by Kito and Ling Productions

For Adults:

www.loginthesoul.com

Echoes of a Vision of Paradise, If You Cannot Remember, You Will Return, Volume 1.

Echoes of a Vision of Paradise, If You Cannot Remember, You Will Return, Volume 2.

Echoes of a Vision of Paradise, If You Cannot Remember, You Will Return, Volume 3.

Echoes of a Vision of Paradise, If You Cannot Remember, You Will Return, a Synopsis (Also available as Audio Book).

Restoring the Heart

The Simulator, A dream within a Dream.

The 2094 Sanction

A Being of Light, God's Will and Pleasure.

Paradise, The Science of the Love of God.

Experiences and Insights

The Key

For Children:

www.loginthesoul.com

Titles and Brief Descriptions

Andy Ant and Beatrice Bee (With a Bonus Coloring Section).

Beauty is on the Inside (With a Bonus Coloring Section).

Bee and Fairy Power (Super-fairies, Bees, and Organic Farmers team up to save Nature and Humanity).

Fly, Fly, Louie Louie (A Story of Change and Identity. With a Bonus Coloring Section).

Grandma and I / Mi Abuelita y Yo (A Bilingual English/Spanish Story, with a Bonus Coloring and Drawing Section).

How Alexander the Gnome Found the Sun (With a Bonus Coloring Section).

Igor's Walkabout (With a Bonus Coloring Section).

Katie Caterpillar Finds Her Song (With a Bonus Coloring Section; also available as Audio Book).

Return to Paradise (Happy the Bluebird and Bright-Wings the Cardinal use Virtues to restore the Professor's Home).

Saving Lantern's Waterfall (An Eco-Adventure).

The King and the Castle (Love Flies in on the Wings of Destiny. With a Bonus Coloring Section).

The Language of Love: Twelve Bilingual Plays Teaching Virtues, for Children to Perform (Accompanying Book for Return to Paradise). In English and Spanish.

Printed in the United States
By Bookmasters